Costume and Design for Devised and Physical Theatre

To h

Costume and Design for Devised and Physical Theatre

TINA BICÂT

THE CROWOOD PRESS

First published in 2012 by
The Crowood Press Ltd
Ramsbury, Marlborough
Wiltshire SN8 2HR

www.crowood.com

British Library Cataloguing-in-Publication Data
A catalogue record for this book is available from the British Library.

ISBN 978 1 84797 372 6

Front cover: Ockham's Razor in *Memento Mori*. (Photo: Nik Mackey)
Frontispiece: RedCape Theatre in *1, Beach Road*. (Photo: Nik Mackey)

Acknowledgements

Thanks to the companies who have let me use photographs of their productions: Chris Baldwin Theatre, Bicat Co., Jonathan Lunn Dance Company, Lost Banditos, NIE, Ockham's Razor, Punchdrunk, RedCape Theatre, St Mary's University College at Strawberry Hill, Theatre-Rites, Turtle Key Arts. And to Chris Baldwin, Patrick Baldwin, Lisette Barlow, Sophie Bellin, Kate Bicât, Nick Bicât, Tony Bicât, Alex Byrne, Lionel Caujolle, Meline Danielevitz, Stefano Di Renzo, Maxine Doyle, Stuart Glover, Christophe Grenier, Mark Griffin, Alex Harvey, Marion Huard, Christine Jarvis, Ali King, Tina Koch, Christine Lee, Nik Mackey, Alexander McDonnell, Polly McDonnell, Alistair Milne, Charlotte Mooney, Sabina Netherclift, Gemma Palomar Delgardo, Ann-Noelle and David Pinnegar at Hammerwood Park, Kate Rigby, Anami Schrijvers, Paul Stowe, Kasper Svenstrup Hansen, Kim Swaden-Ward, Trevor Walker, Kasia Zeremba Byrne and all the people with whom I work, and who have answered my questions. Photos and drawings are by the author unless otherwise stated.

'He' and 'she' are used indiscriminately in this book because, of course, everyone in this job does everything they can.

For Jessie and Felix Caujolle and Daisy and Tom McDonnell, with my love.

Typeset by Phoenix Typesetting, Auldgirth, Dumfriesshire
Printed and bound in Singapore by Craft Print International

Contents

1 The World of Devised and Physical Theatre

A set that suggests a world and leaves room for actors and objects to invent. (Photo: Kasia Zeremba Byrne)

Doing the Splits in Tight Trousers

There's a difficult meeting point when performers, who perhaps are somersaulting six metres above the stage,

Theatre-Rites and Ockham's Razor in *Hang On*. (Photo: Patrick Baldwin)

want to play everyday people. They need to play recognizable characters and tell real stories while performing dangerous feats which no ordinary human could manage in skin-tight lycra, let alone in a suit and tie which might flap and catch, come untucked and rip.

How can a dancer perform an arabesque in a Victorian skirt that appears to weigh several kilos? How can you

(Photo: Nik Mackey)

(Photo: Nik Mackey)

(Photo: Alex Byrne)

Costumes are not solely for actors to wear; sometimes they can become an integral part of the set.

(Photo: Alex Byrne)

(Photo: Lisette Barlow)

(Photo: Lisette Barlow)

do a back flip in a hooded jacket without the hood falling over your face and blinding you for the all-important landing? What happens to the librarian's specs when she is flying on the end of a rope, or walking on her hands in her dream of a more exciting life? What happens to the fairy's wings in the rain?

These, and hundreds of other problems, present themselves during the design and making process of any production that calls for unusual movement or circumstance. Many of them are not apparent before rehearsals start because most of this sort of work is created through the devising process in the rehearsal room. But it is a great help to be prepared, and to invent designs that are sympathetic to the physical needs of the performer.

It is easy to forget, in the busy and engrossing work of making theatre, how much work the audience does in interpreting what they see and hear. They can be made up of theatrically experienced people and those who have never been to a performance before. We may put our ideas on the stage for them to see, but they interpret them each in their own particular way using their own particular experience and interest. Our ideas, which seem so solid and important to us as we turn them into words and music, sights and sounds, are only suggestions, and we have to trust the audience to enlarge them into reality.

The Setting and the Light

The setting in which the performers play their parts is the first thing that the audience sees, and helps their understanding of, and involvement in, the show. It gives people confidence that their interpretation is on the right lines, or tells them if they can allow their mind to create a more abstract world. The set is the frame and the context for the costume designer's work. Physical theatre tends to make the most of any available stage space for the movement of the actors. The setting has to allow for this, which can mean that there is not much room for the actual set, and the costume and objects or props have to work together with the lighting to do the set's

job. The performers and the lighting designer are the people who give it life.

Without light the world that the designer makes for the performers and the audience is lifeless. In a controlled theatre space, where the light of any mood and place can be created, the audience's attention is focused directly on the action. In the open air in the daytime the designer has to design for God's lighting, which is less reliable though often no less theatrical. The first consideration will be the quality of the natural light. This depends on the country, the time of day, and where the sun is in the sky at the time of the performance. In some parts of the world this is reliable – for example July in the South of France is usually flooded with light. Northern climates can be more problematic, however, and colour has to be clear enough to show up in a grey, soft light if nature does not choose to give you the light you hope for when you want it.

Collaborative Company Design

RESEARCH AND DEVELOPMENT

Rehearsals for a devised performance are not the same as those for a performance that is script led. It is quite usual for this rehearsal period to be a research and development ('R & D') time. This means that the end result of this particular period will be either a short, rudimentary performance, possibly to attract future funding, or a springboard to the discussions and development of the finished work. These sessions are invaluable to the designer. The cast may not be the final choice for the performance, and much of the content will be unformed and experimental. But the style the company will work in, the atmosphere they hope to create on stage, and the reality or otherwise of the world they are inventing, will be clear.

There will have been meetings, and perhaps casting workshops, before this collaborative creative period. The company will have been chosen not only for their skill, but also for their inventive ability. It can take a long time to assemble a company, and often a nucleus of the group will have worked together before and will have a

All theatre technicians love gaffer tape (duct tape) and cable ties.

tried and tested working relationship; new members will have been chosen for their ability to fit in with the group and to add fresh skills to the process. Designers for each production are chosen for the same reasons; their differing skills and particular specializations must be appropriate to the style of work envisaged.

The design of all areas used in the production will grow together. The number of different designers employed on a show varies with the scale of the production and its budget. Designers and makers who work in this field tend to have an open ability to design anything that appears on a stage, and particular skill in one or two fields. The costume designer for a devised production may also be responsible for the design of the set, effects, props or objects. If puppets and masks are being used they will be in her design brief unless other people with these particular skills have been employed.

Skills tend to overlap. A physical theatre company devising a piece may include actors who are also musicians, dancers, acrobats or puppeteers. Performers are trained in a wide variety of skills and know that their best chance of success in the ever-changing world of theatre is to have a wide base of expertise to draw on. The company may use one person in a variety of ways. An actor may make puppets and show others how to animate them, or use a specialized skill in movement for mask work, stage fighting or tumbling. Designers working in this type of theatre need a similar variety of chameleon skills.

COLLABORATION

A devising company will make decisions collaboratively. The designer's vision encompasses the whole production as the audience will see it. Performers often have a

An improvised costume sets the design for the performance. (Photos: Alex Byrne)

picture in their head of the way they will look as a character, but their situation prevents them from imagining the production as a whole, or how they will look within it. It is important, therefore, that you all work together quickly and openly near the beginning of the rehearsal period, before actors' visions become too fixed and engrained into their character development and movement, or yours into a characterization that does not exist.

In every department, through each stage of making a production, there runs a difficulty. So much is invented by so many different people, all of whom have been employed because of the skill, the speed and the variety of their invention, but not all of their improvisations and ideas can make it to the final production. Many will be followed and will perhaps have taken a long time to develop, and it can be hard for everyone to recognize, at the end of all this labour, that they have been sweating down a blind alley. One of the great skills of this type of rehearsal is to recognize these *culs de sac* early, to drop an idea without regret or personal involvement, and then to get on with the job. Another is to find the way to communicate an idea clearly and excitingly enough for it to get a fair trial.

Performers improvising with costume can be astonishingly quick in inventing characters and action around any costume or objects they are given to work with. The imaginations and inventions of a devising company can produce a dozen ideas from the same source, and an actor may show you depths and movement in a costume that surprise and delight you. On the other hand, they can also fail to notice possibilities in a costume because they are playing within it, rather than seeing it from the outside, as you are. Performer and designer, when they can work together from both points of view, get the best results from any costume.

Group discussion will be easier if you have talked about your reactions to the initial stimulus with the director before rehearsals start, and perhaps have pinned up a few images or produced some hats or small items that are appropriate to this germ of a concept. These and the concept they suggest can be discarded at the first discussion, but at least there will be something concrete

to work from. Rudimentary on-the-spot sketches will describe your thoughts to the company more clearly than words.

Another useful skill is to draw as someone describes the costume they imagine, so that you can both see what is in each other's mind; later, in the more peaceful situation of your workroom, you can translate these scribbles into complete drawings and add to them with appropriate images.

THE PLACE OF THE DESIGNER IN THE COMPANY

The designer in this sort of group has the opportunity to invent and present suggestions and solutions, which can help the company work through the process. How they do it is different for every company and every project. Everyone in the devising workroom is there to help invent the final performance, and all share the responsibility for the development of the work.

In the world of devised, physical theatre it is quite usual for the designer to be a maker, too. This is partly a matter of the budget, but even where there is enough money to employ more people, it is better for the designer to stay closely in touch with the changing and inventive progress of the work. A drawing of a costume invented through rehearsal can be given to an outside maker, but in order to really understand how the costume must be cut, the maker must see the actor moving in rehearsal and spend time with the designer understanding their ideas. If rehearsal results in a new aspect having to be incorporated into the costume, the designer must redesign, and the whole business begins again. It is possible to work like this, and many people do, but unless designer and maker know each other's work very well it will be a time-consuming affair.

Makers at Work

Once a designer and her makers have worked together a few times, a team style will be established, and a sort of shorthand can develop where everyone's skills are used to the best advantage of the project. It may be that the designer is an excellent cutter, an impatient shopper,

Make sure the company know which are stand-in costumes and props and which are performance ones.

Maker at work.

an adequate fitter and a slipshod seamstress. She will choose a team that includes people with the missing skills. This means that makers, with all their abilities in shopping, dying or cutting, have a much greater input into the work than in a non-devised piece. The better they understand the needs of the company, the demands of the movement and the eyes of the designer, the closer they will come to being assistant designers, rather than straightforward makers. They will often become a familiar and trusted presence in the rehearsal room, and make decisions or suggestions with great freedom.

The Devising Process

For those not familiar with the process of devising, a rough guide might be helpful. It can only be rough because every company has their own way of working, and every project its own stages and momentum.

First idea for a production: This can come from anywhere – a conversation overheard on a bus or a wish to change the world.

Sharing the idea: Opening out the idea in words or in

writing is the first step towards the public ear and eye of an audience.

Beginning research: Putting flesh on the bones of an idea through a search for appropriate and inspiring research and conversation.

Funding: Working out how to pay for rehearsals and production.

Choosing the company: Collecting a creative team whose members will work together and have an appropriate variety of skills both in their specialization and their ability to work together as a company.

Research and development (R&D): Testing and developing the idea and the company skills. Also used for casting, and collecting material to attract funding.

Development: Further work away from the rehearsal room to develop the idea, the style, the company make-up and the funding.

When and where and who: Settling the dates and venues of rehearsals and performances; also checking the

A Design Game for Rehearsal and Improvisation

There is game played by children all over the world. It may be called 'Grandmother's footsteps', 'Babushka' or 'Un, deux, trois, Soleil!' but it has the same rules: one person stands in front with their back to the rest of the group, which is as far away as is practical. The group has to creep up on the 'Grandmother', who will whisk round every few seconds and try to catch them moving. If she sees them they have to go back to the beginning and start again. The winner is the first person to touch 'Grandmother'. The game becomes a fiercely concentrated and often very comic game of skill when played by physical performers with trained bodies and minds, and every sense alert to performance possibilities. Adding an element of dressing up to this game presents a whole new platform for comic invention.

Between the performers and 'Grandmother' there is a barrier made up of a heap of costumes and props. This may look random, but has been carefully chosen to include items that can be worn by many different sizes and in many different ways.

The game is now more difficult. The actors have to dress up without their movement being seen. As the game continues a strange collection of characters begins to emerge. At some point the director may see the possibility of a connection between two or three of these characters, and may make a pause in the game while they develop a short improvisation. Then the game resumes, perhaps with the improvisation being remembered for future development.

The designer can take away items that are either stereotyping the characters in a way that is not helpful, or add items that will enrich the ideas, or to help her see the way particular performers work in different clothes. An actor wearing a full skirt which will swing from the hips with every turn will move very differently to one in a crossover flowered overall or a white laboratory coat with pockets. A surprise prop in one of the pockets – a lipstick in a case and a small hand mirror, a photograph of a child in a locket, a broken watch – could result in a morning of new invention. If

Improvisation with costume leads to the final design for performance. (Photos 1, 3 to 6: Kasia Zeremba Byrne; photo 2: Alex Byrne)

availability of the chosen company, and contracting them to the work.

Rehearsals: Schedules and venues.

Performance: With luck leading to success, future performances and development of the company.

It all sounds so clear and simple when set out on paper.

Clothes often look very different inside-out.

the surprise is appropriate to the path of the story, the work is more likely to be useful to the eventual production.

The *dramatis personae* and sights that develop could never be planned on paper in the studio on imagined bodies. The incompatibility of colour, style and shape will be extreme. Gender and personalities cross and appear in a way that is dictated by the strictures of the game's rules, and not by probability or sensible, researched planning. The designer will see ideas outside the combinations of colour and shape that have been tried and tested, and may find new inspiration in the wild improbability of the sights she sees. She will also see the way the actors wear the odd costumes, and how a certain cut or colour of cloth or pair of spectacles lends an air and a posture to a particular performer – or the spark that will help him reveal, through the magic and skill of his work, the unteachable, unexplainable trick that makes people look at him, listen to him, and care about his story.

Each step, apart from the first and last which are clear in their single-minded simplicity, leads to a huge and open space full of people, possibility, hazard and invention. The project can falter and fail, or fly and succeed at any one of them. Each stage has to be in place to pass to the next. Many of the stages on this journey are so interesting and involving that even if the funding fails and the performance never happens, the interest of the creation

Shoelaces are good for more than shoes because of their strength and stiff ends for threading.

The actor's body and the shadow puppet work together to make the wolf climb the stairs. (Photo: Nik Mackey)

process remains and the nucleus of the company will try again on another project, or develop the initial idea in another form.

Different Specializations

PUPPET MAKING

The designing and making of puppets is one of the unplanned and unbudgeted tasks that often fall within the brief of the costume designer and maker in devised small-scale theatre. No one might have known in advance that they would feel the need of a puppet, and consequently no one would have been included in the company with that specialized skill. The safest way to approach creating a puppet that will become one with its animator, who may well have never worked with puppets before, is to start tentatively. You need to find a path towards the most natural way for the actor to work with the puppet, and make sure that you are capable of designing and making an object that will give all the right messages to the audience. It is no good

creating a beautiful, complex marionette if the actor doesn't have the specialized skill of giving it life, and no good imagining a puppet that you do not have the skill, equipment or budget to create. This does not mean the puppet in the show won't be full of life and vigour.

As the scene begins to develop in rehearsal you can begin to experiment with the actor and director with different types of puppet and objects to discover what feels most natural and telling in the circumstance. A sock or a glove on a hand will give the feeling of a glove puppet, and a rolled-up newspaper, crumpled and taped into shape, will suggest a more complex body and its movement. Knotted cloth, or a ball on crossed sticks with an old shirt will promote a different type of work. Once you see how the actor is working, you can start refining these rough suggestions into forms, which will eventually assume the character and movement of the puppet's character in the performance.

The only rule is that the puppet is able, with the actor's help, to give the messages of its character and actions to the audience; how and with what you create it does not matter: if it works, it's good.

You can buy bladed needles for sewing leather, which are useful for other tough work.

A collection of masks made by different methods.

MASKS

Mask making is a specialized skill, and working in masks takes particular training. This does not prevent them turning up unexpectedly in a devised production, and much of the training of physical performers means that they find it easy to adapt to the restrictions of movement and facial expression that masks demand of bodies; they are used to absorbing emotion and fact and showing it through the movement of their bodies, and this particularly theatrical device does not limit them in the same way as it does more naturalistically trained performers.

Once again, the best way to proceed is to get some masks into rehearsal as soon as possible so that you can establish the style of mask that will be best for the production and the performers. There are basic questions that need to be answered straightaway. For example, do the actors have to talk or sing in the masks? If so, the mouth must be clear or the mask formed to allow the sound out. Are the masks blank and the character provided by the movement, or do they give the character to the actor who creates the movement from the way the mask makes him feel? Once the director has decided on a style of mask and play, then it is time to create a prototype, which will lead to the finished article.

There are always problems when actors start working in masks as they are usually hot and uncomfortable. Many fitting problems can be alleviated by gluing slivers of foam to the inside of the mask's forehead to take away the pressure on the nose and its bridge, and making sure that the eyeholes are set in exactly the right place and that the actor's eyelashes are not encumbered by the eyeholes when he blinks. The closer the eyeholes are to the eyes, the better the actor's peripheral vision.

Many devised performances go on growing and changing throughout their life, particularly if they are being performed night after night in the same venue. This can be because a change of performer during a long run may present the company with a different skill that could be incorporated into the show. Performers who work in the devised and physical side of performance have different skills. Though replacements would be cast for a similar ability to perform the rehearsed work, they might have different secondary skills, which could be used in the performance. The violin-playing ability of one performer may replace the splendid singing voice of another, or a trick cyclist replace a juggler. Costumes may have to be redesigned and made for these changes whilst keeping the balance of the rest of the concept intact.

2 Invention in the Rehearsal Room

Different Approaches

Performance that is created not from a script but through collaborative work in the rehearsal room presents particular challenges to the designer. The excitement in the opportunity to invent and improvise the costume side by side with the actors and director far outweighs the fact that rehearsals are often infuriating and exhausting, and call for much patient, silent participation. Work where the company collaborates in this sort of process has a wave-like rhythm. There are times when all flows easily and almost effortlessly and ideas coalesce without problem – and there are times when it feels as if you are wading through treacle, and when a wave that is full of power and potential just refuses to break and give up its secrets. The designer has the opportunity, in these moments, to produce inventive solutions, which give new inspiration and confidence to the process.

THE DESIGNER'S VIEWPOINT

Designers can read a script and use their skill, research and imagination to support the invention of the writer and the concept of the director. They can pull information from the words on the pages and work with the director and the rest of the creative team to bring the page to life. The arc of the narrative will be in place; the characters will exist in the words written for them to say and the context the author has created for their lives.

NIE in *Tales from the Sea Journey*. (Photo: Alex Byrne)

Much of the subsequent design work is spent alone in research and in the studio so that a model of the set and a batch of costume designs can be shown to the company on the first day of rehearsal. Everyone has a good idea of what they will be wearing before they begin to move as their characters.

None of these facts may be in place before the first rehearsal of a devised piece. All the designer may bring to the company on that first day may be a pencil and an empty sketchbook. The bulk of the invention is sparked by the action in the rehearsal room and design ideas are developed publicly and collaboratively. The quiet time in the studio often becomes a late night scrabble to make practical sense of the inventions of the day in time for the next day's rehearsal. The designer's picture begins to grow at the first introduction to the stimulus, usually some time before the first rehearsal. The details of it will come from the improvisation and movement of the performer.

Dance, drama, physical theatre and community work all need design. It is not just a case of the audience seeing something beautiful: the visual effects help place the work in a context, give the characters depth and rigour, and underline and support the emotional content of the work. The nature of devised work lets a designer work with the director and performer to build the characters and the place of the story, and to work right at the hub of the process.

The value of this invention stems from its viewpoint. Performers, however generous and imaginative, are not in a position to watch their own performance. Directors must consider the work from a range of different

Early work on a scripted performance… (Photo: Christine Jarvis)

…and on a devised show. (Photo: David Hockham)

viewpoints and their input is usually vocal and considered. A designer's most important sense is sight, and a visual response is their instinctive and first reaction. The ideas that tumble into your head when you imagine a situation are pictures. This makes you useful in a collaborative rehearsal, as long as you can manage to explain those ideas, because no one else in the room is looking from your uncomplicated viewpoint, except possibly the

Many actors do not know where their waist is – do not trust their own measurements.

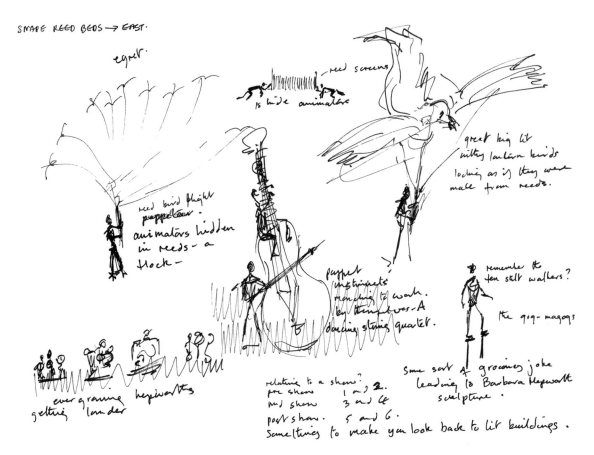

Notes from an early discussion of a project.

lighting or sound designer if they are there. You become the eyes of the audience.

THE VISUAL ASPECT OF PHYSICAL WORK

The body's movement, and the way it uses the performance space and reacts with other bodies, give costume design for physical performance a particular importance. The genre, often without words or a narrative line, has a more abstract quality than most scripted work, and uses the way that people react instinctively to light, silhouette and colour in a direct and demanding way. Think of the traditional but still used ballet dancer's tutu: it leads the audience to see a tiny waist, fragile, bare shoulders looking more tender than ever above the crisp, light-catching wheel of the skirt and the long, slim length of leg extended by the *pointe* shoes. The dancer bends to touch her pointed toe, and the grace of the line of her body is extended by the upward tilt of her skirt behind her.

The audience do not think about this illusion any more than they think of the muscles, sweat, and pain; they see an unearthly beauty floating in the white spotlight. It's a very different matter in the harsh light of the rehearsal room when layers of well worn vests, knee pads, elastic supports and legwarmers show the difficulty of the job.

Both outfits have surprising similarities as work wear. The shoulders are free, the line of the arms and neck uncluttered, and the movement of the hips and ankles is unrestricted. The clown's costume of huge, baggy trousers and enormous shoes serves the same purpose, as does the sparkling bodysuit of the trapeze artist. These traditional costumes have developed and stay with us as symbols of a particular type of performance, though they say little about the character of the role. Their

Dramatic stripes turn these three clowns into a chorus. (Photo: Lisette Barlow)

theatricality hides the fact that they are working dress, and that whatever the costumes look like, if the performer cannot work in them they are useless.

The style of most physical theatre work is less rigid than ballet and the costume less rigid than the tutu, but they are both designed not only for their effect on the audience, but also to allow and enhance the quality of movement in the work. It is vital that the design does not limit this in any way, and is a constant danger in both the design and the making of the costumes. Imagine lifting your leg above your head and then think how much more difficult it would be with the weight of a kilo or two of velvet hanging from it in the form of a skirt. But as a designer you might long for the royal richness of light and depth of colour that velvet would give.

Balancing these decisions, and finding ways to give both audience and performer the best experience, is a skill that needs careful thought, discussion and imagination. You can't make decisions like this without seeing the sort of movement that is being created in rehearsal. And you can't tell how the performer is most at ease in their clothes until you see the way they use their body to express their feelings.

THE VALUE OF CHAT, WATCHING, AND REHEARSAL CLOTHES

The value of chat to discover the points people love or hate about clothes cannot be overestimated. Performers, like all humans, are happiest and most physically and emotionally confident when they feel they look good in their clothes and right in their bodies. Even people who are not particularly conscious of their personal appearance like to feel comfortable. Physical performance is often exhausting and sometimes dangerous, and the designer must make it possible for its players to forget what they look like and concentrate on their job. For this to happen they must trust the designer's judgement. It is not surprising that it takes time for this trust and easy communication to be established, and the designer's presence in rehearsals, and his ability to see his work from the performers' as well as the audiences' point of view takes time, talk, and a certain flexibility in decision making.

If breasts stay in a low cut bodice in a backbend, they will probably stay in through any other activity.

You can tell a lot from the sort of clothes that the performers choose to wear for rehearsal. Some may like tops that cling tight to the body, while others prefer a floppy shirt. There are people who like to work wearing as little as possible, and others who have layers of an assortment of t-shirts, vests, leggings, sweaters, hats and tracksuit bits. People dress for comfort and practicality, and there's a charming lack of personal vanity in the room once the work gets going. This frankness shows a designer the cut of costume that helps a performer to work his best. The challenge is to use that cut in a costume that also tells the audience the story of the character without limiting the actor's instinctive freedom of movement.

Stimuli

With regard to the practical application of visual and tactile stimuli, there is no limit to starting points for devised work, and no limit to the number of directions in which a company can go when they begin to devise round a subject.

STORY

The most common way for a devised production, physical or otherwise, to begin its life is a true or fictional story. Everyone has the same story to read, and the whole company can start their creative experience for a show from the same point. The designer's reaction to the story, and their interest and previous knowledge of the world it shows, is the start of their design process. The images that present themselves in the mind depend on the information already stored in the brain. Consequently a designer who has interest and experience in physics will have a different reaction to a biography of Isaac Newton than a designer who has a particular interest in the costume and manners of eighteenth-century England. Their starting point for research will differ – one will instantly see the whirling particles of gravitational pull in the white light of science,

An image that could provoke a dozen stories. (Photo: Marie Rosendhal Chemnitz)

It may be useful for outdoor rehearsal to have some old gym mats to cut up for actors to stand on; they will stay warmer.

The formal world of the eighteenth century re-imagined for a devised theatre production. (Photo: Christine Jarvis)

and the other the frock coat and wig in warm candle-light; the development of their work and decision-making must come from both sources. Research will change the way they see the story's world as their memory stores up new information and visual images.

A SCRIPTED PLAY

A physical theatre reworking of some aspects of a scripted play combines the traditional techniques of using character-based costume design with the techniques of designing and cutting for movement. In a play the characters are there. They have pasts, and live their lives in a world that has already been created by the author who invented them. However, they are altered by the devising process, which often stresses only a single aspect of their character or experience, even though they remain at heart the people who spoke the lines written on the page. This gives the designer a character to imagine at the start of the design process. The future development of these pictures will change them, but the starting point exists.

MUSIC

The power of music lies close to the instigation of much physical work. The reaction of humans to music is universal. It is close to the inventive drive of those to whom the movement of their own or other people's bodies through the air is a language. The difficulty of using music as an initial stimulus for a project is that humans have such different reactions when they hear it. Despite this it always has an uncluttered truth at its heart.

A designer does not have to like the music that inspires the work to understand the emotional content of the tones and rhythms within it, and to use them to guide the tones and rhythms of their images. These instinctive reactions, used by the designer in their invention of stage pictures, are particularly useful for physical work, as they will connect closely with those of the movement director.

POLITICS AND HISTORY

Many instigators of devised projects have a strong impetus to bring the attention of the audience to a wide range of political and historical situations. The costume designer's initial preparation for such work is to make sure of the clothes people wear or wore in the real life

Check whether it will be daylight or dark at the show time of an open-air performance; things can look very different out of stage-light.

Suggestions Box

Specific to era	*1950s*	Women's hats	Handbag with powder compact and lipstick	Nylon stockings with seams	Telephone with dial
Specific to place	*Hospital*	Patient's gown	Doctor's coat	Oxygen mask	Syringe
Specific to age	*Childhood*	Small soft blanket	Super-hero cloak or princess skirt	Soft toy	Comic or book from the appropriate era

Clothes and accessories from the 1950s collected to nudge the memory.

situations to be explored. The development of their design will depend on the way the director wants to use the political information for the work. The costume will often have to reflect a reality recognizable to the audience, such as an army uniform, and the designer must recreate a uniform that will work with the physical style of movement. In many cases this means that the design will provoke the audiences' imaginations to re-create the detail of images they already know from the less accurate images they see on the actors on stage.

Verbatim and reminiscence theatre take their inspiration directly from conversations and stories told by people who have lived through an experience, and performances are devised using people's stories as the starting block of an idea. Much of the impetus for this genre of performance comes from memories and life

The Application of Stimuli

Virginia Woolf, the writer, committed suicide in 1941, after years of struggle with episodes of madness, by weighting her pockets with stones and wading into a river. This bleak biographical fact contains within it resonances that could instigate very different pieces of work depending on the interests of the different creative theatre practitioners who read it, and the styles in which they work. For example:

The director might imagine an exploration of Virginia Woolf's life playing out as she drowns, running parallel to a wider abstract dance piece choreographing the irresistible attraction of death.

The movement director/choreographer might imagine the slow determination of the woman's walk to her death and the change of her bodyweight as she wades deeper and deeper until her whole weight is held and moved by the water.

The dramaturge might think of the back story in the life of the woman: her bouts of creativity and madness, the interest and passions of her writings, and the biography of her past life that led to this moment, and absorb her despair into a story.

The composer/sound designer might hear the water sliding through the sounds of the countryside and imagine the changes as the woman's ears get nearer and nearer the surface of the water, the way it might sound as she sinks beneath it, and perhaps a snatch of her past in the ghost of a melody.

The set designer might consider only the complications of suggesting the land and water of the scene on stage, and imagine the colours of early spring in rural Sussex, the textures of lanes, fields and trees, and the slope of the river bank as she wades through the shallows into deep, fast-running water.

The lighting designer might see just the colour of the light on the country riverbank, and the play of light on the moving water, and imagine the magnification of light on the weeds and the floating body below its surface.

The costume designer might see only the shape of the skirt and the loose cardigan jacket, both of which will indicate to the audience the era of the story and the social class of the woman, and the heavy drop of the lines of the clothes caused by the weight of the stones in the pockets. Other thoughts will run parallel: the texture of wet tweed and damp leather, the colours suggested by despair, and the lines of the cut of the clothes suggesting the depth of the sorrow in the story.

The puppet and object maker might imagine the waterweed and rushes bending with the current, and the fish and the swimming life and water movement below the surface.

The way the work develops in preparation and rehearsal will determine whether any of these ideas are used, and which ones may be appropriate for the aspect of the story the director wants to work on. The combination of the ways in which different creative artists react to facts is one of the factors that make devised theatre so rich in possibility.

stories of the company or community which are shared, selected, honed and woven into a performance which may develop and travel far from its origins. The ideas may be crafted into a script, in which case the design brief would be the same as for any other naturalistic, scripted show. But if the stories are to be choreographed into a dance, or woven into a stylized piece of physical theatre, which has grown from the seeds of these memories or real-life events, the costume designer may play a more active part in the creation of the work. Those taking part – often in these stories not actors but members of the local community – can be asked to bring an item of clothing or an object that connects with their experience and their memories.

Do not forget the sound a costume makes if you are designing for a small or miked venue.

NUDGING AND FREEING MEMORY WITH REMINDERS OF THE PAST

Older people do not always consider their past experiences to be particularly valuable or interesting to a younger generation, or even know how much they remember. The designer can help by offering clothes and objects which might kickstart the stories. Most women, even if they cannot remember what they wore yesterday, can remember their first adult party as clearly as they can remember the music of their youth. How many objects, and how closely applicable they are to the work, depends on the subject and the budget. Old memories of a wartime childhood may be revived by the sight and feel of a gas mask in its case, a pair of 1940s child's braces or knickers, or a headscarf tied in a certain way. These prosaic objects can start a train of memories, and help people to talk and act openly, and a designer to begin the process of creating a context for the work with costume and objects. And they open in front of the costume researcher a brightly lit, untouched window on a world that has passed.

FACTS AND ABSTRACTS

A wider or more abstract first stimulus may be the starting point for a piece of work. It could be factual, such as erosion or the power of language, or more intangible, such as breath or mania. In these cases the designer has to discover from the director which aspect of these stimuli it is that attracts his interest and makes him want to develop a piece of work around the subject. This is easier to find out with the more factually based ideas, because buried under the abstraction there will be some story or experience that can become a starting point for conversation.

The more abstract ideas will be based in fact, but these are much harder to discover since they can look completely different when considered from different aspects. Breath could work as a sound and movement which is the basis of all life and death, or as the biography of a runner, or a hundred other ideas, and you cannot really begin to think about your designs at all until you know the director's point of view.

A jumble assortment of costumes and props being used to develop a scene. (Photo: David Hockham)

Early Rehearsals

The first sight of the rehearsal room of a physical theatre performance company is rather like opening the door to a bizarre playroom. People are changing their clothes, or they are already dressed in an eccentric assortment of training clothes, ranging from neat Lycra gymwear to floppy tracksuit remnants and woolly hats. Most people have bare feet and are on the move, warming and stretching their muscles with floor exercise. Instead of the neat piles of scripts on a circle of chairs the room is bordered by small heaps of clothes and musical instruments, and the bottles of water and bananas that everyone there uses to keep them going during the day.

The room is full of noise and chatter. Actor/musicians

Make sure guitar straps and the like are congenial to the rest of the design.

may be playing in a private space separated from the mayhem by nothing more than their concentration on the sounds they are making. The stage manager's careful coloured tape mark-out of the parameters of a pre-designed set on the floor is replaced by the cheerful chalk lines marking the court of a ball game. The director may well be rolling around the floor with everyone else, while technicians organize their equipment in small areas of calm.

The stuff being unpacked and sorted by the designer in the room may look as random as everything else lying around, like a cross between a table at a jumble sale and a miniature workshop. But the tumbled assortment, even though it looks so unstructured, will be a carefully considered collection of clothes and objects, which will help the director and actors in their invention. The work-shop will have the simple tools that could help change the nature of the objects to follow or lead the path of improvisations; a sweater taped on to a stick can stand in for a flag, or an umbrella wired to a lump of foam rubber and a belt for a machine gun.

GAMES

At some point the room will quieten and the whole company will gather into a circle on the floor to hear about and discuss the proposed path of the day's work. The warm-up work which follows will be more structured and involve everyone working together; its purpose is to concentrate the energy and alertness of the company to the work that is to come. The games that are used to do this need combinations of intense physical, mental and vocal attention and hone the skills the performers need to be aware of themselves and each other during the working day.

These games give the costume designer an opportunity that is rare in scripted work. They allow her to watch the natural movements and similarities and contrasts of the bodies and rhythms of the performers – information that no measurements or photos can convey – before she designs the costume. The performers will be wearing the undisguised supports or bandages that help their bodies cope with recurrent injuries. The heartbeat rhythm and

connection with the floor and the air that they naturally fall into will be displayed as their bodies are forgotten and their concentration narrows to the game they are playing. A design opportunity may emerge from these sessions that you could never imagine in the studio: a comic relationship between the light-rhythmed, soft-springing, open-palmed man and the earthy-hipped, angled-elbowed, confident stability of the blond-haired woman, an unexpectedly boyish grace in an elderly clown, the sudden ability of a girl to turn from a quick-silver flirt to a skinny old crone.

Choices of cut, colour and texture begin to grow from the actors' movement and bodily rhythms. The audience

The company work as a chorus with a single more specific character. (Photo: Lisette Barlow)

Keep an extension lead with your tool kit.

will never know, and the company may never discover why you watch them so closely, but they will feel it at their first costume fitting when the clothes, however different they look from their usual style of dress, feel right on their bodies.

The Day's Work

The rhythm of the day's work will follow this pattern of periods of intense physical invention and times of reflection on the development and refining of the improvised work. Much of the improvised work will be dismissed and forgotten; some of it will be noted and discussed and worked on again. There are always some ideas which, though tempting and full of possibility, are not helpful to the path of the work or appropriate to the style of direction. It is worth keeping a note of these for future projects.

The development of a costume design that gives character may grow later. Devised physical work often begins from a point where the company works as a kind of chorus. Characters emerge from improvisation as people step out of the chorus, invent round a theme and become a major player in its story. These improvisations, which may use anything lying around as props or costume, start to influence the character of a costume.

A piece of music may be played that suggests a Balkan party. The performers, as a chorus, will begin to become the people at the party and may grab water bottles to stand in as wine, tie a scarf, gypsy fashion, round their heads or use a sweater as a shawl. They will do this because it helps their bodies feel more like the character they imagine in their heads. A successful stand-in costume may lead to one or two players stepping out from the group to become, for a few minutes, major players in the scene. These gimcrack costumes are clues to this connection, which can be used in the designer's subsequent work on the costume.

The close collaboration between devising performers and their creative team is one of the strongest elements in the design process for devised theatre, making it so different from that of a scripted play or choreographed dance piece. The other is the requirement that the dramaturgy, sound, lighting and visual design, and all the other production issues such as budget, publicity and casting, give as much freedom as possible to allow for invention and physicality in rehearsal. The strand that stays the same in all sorts of performance is that the work is for the audience, and the design, along with all other elements, will ultimately improve their experience and enlighten their understanding when they see the show.

3 Communication and Meetings

The Designer's Place in the Team

Costume, set and object design, lighting and sound are linked in any physical theatre production, and they build upon each other's inspiration in a closely collaborative way. It may be that the costume designer's job is to give the lighting and sound designer a picture that they can bring to life with their particular arts. Imagine a train platform, with a tunnel at one end, packed with commuters on their way to work. This could, with the sound and lighting adding to the image, be a scene of grinding grey despair at the bleakness of life. But with golden light flooding through the tunnel at the end of the platform and music suggesting revelation and hope, the same performers in the same costumes on the same set could be at the doors of heaven. The costume designer needs to make sure that the creators of these effects have the right palette to work on: not too many colours that stand out, a crispness and variety of silhouette rather than colour.

Then imagine that the musical story at this station follows a group of football supporters on their way to a match. The bright team colours they wear must contrast with the colours of the rest of the performers so that when they form into a choir on the platform they create a solid block of contrast colour to the other passengers. The lighting designer will focus the audience attention on them by colouring the light to enhance their costumes. Both music and light coming through the tunnel will set the mood, despairing or triumphant, of the supporters. None of this happens automatically; it is the result of discussion and collaboration between all three designers and the director.

All devised projects start with one person's idea and cannot begin to grow until this idea is communicated. How it develops and is eventually given to the public is the difficult bit. The designer is as likely as anybody to start the process and can have as much to do with its development as anyone else in the company. There will be a time near the start of the project when you will have to translate the pictures in your mind into words and images that others will understand.

Meetings

All the many meetings, fascinating or infuriating, which happen in the course of the creation and the life of a production, need planning. In the worst case they will be explosive and trailing with anecdote and an underlying negativity which saps the life of invention. In the best case they give everyone space and opportunity to share ideas, solve problems and plan the cohesive development of the project.

A successful scheduled company or production meeting will always have at its heart an agenda of points to be discussed and someone who, however informally, ensures that everyone who needs to, gets a chance to participate, keeps to the point, and that all the points are covered and noted. The bulk of a designer's input into these meetings may be graphic rather than verbal, and

Ockham's Razor in *The Mill*. (Photo: Nik Mackey)

Technical problems solved during informal meetings.

it helps to make sure you have covered everything you need to communicate by making your own list of things you want to show or talk about, and if possible, where they slot in to the agenda.

Scheduled meetings between one or two members of the creative team may be more informal but are not always easy to manage. Director/designer discussions can go on for days, if there are days to spare in the planning stage of a project, but once the show has reached the rehearsal stage, time and space are short and expensive. Production talks have to be slotted into breaks in rehearsal or between other meetings, and risk being interrupted by phone calls or urgent questions from other sources. Once again the list of things that really must be discussed or decided helps achieve a successful outcome.

Not all meetings are scheduled events round a table. Some of the most valuable ones happen by mistake in the café or corridor, or during the moments when performers are taking a quick break in rehearsal. They are the ones when a designer can snatch a few moments from the director's busy day to clarify a point or show a sketch of a new idea. It is as well to have a clear idea of what you want to say and to make sure it has some relevance to the work that is going on in the room, and does not break the mood or the concentration of the rehearsal. The value of having a designer developing the visual side of a devised production is counteracted by having an extra layer of invention going on during valuable rehearsal time. A designer has to make sure that the work produced during these sessions does not cause more trouble than it is worth. It is best to save complex ideas until the end of the working day to minimize interruption.

All physical work starts with a company warm-up, and this can be a useful slot in the day for a casual meeting with other members of the creative team, and even with the performers. Sensitive observation will enable you to notice when ligaments, muscles and minds demand total or groaning concentration, and the times during this daily ritual when muscles require repetitive or held movement and performers chat amongst themselves. This is your opportunity to snatch an informal meeting. A physical performer may welcome the interest and opportunity, during the repetitive business of stretching a hamstring with their head on their knee, to talk about their costume. It can be better than a scheduled fitting for a discussion of the way the costume will work with the movement, as both designer and performer have their minds on the stretching and shifting limbs. It can also be a good time to note and measure the position and expansion of a muscle during a particular movement: a movement that calls for great physical strength could make many centimetres of difference in the cut of a sleeve or a shoulder, which must be allowed for in the costume design.

Opening the Box

The skill of showing other people, who may have very different interests and imaginations to your own, what is in your head is as important and basic to a designer's job as knowing that green light makes red paint look brown, or that the weight of a cloth affects the way it hangs on the body. But it is much more difficult to learn because the rules change with each job and every group of people you work with.

The way you write your thoughts on an application form for a grant, and the way you scribble and gesture your way to understanding with a fellow designer may seem so different, but they have the same purpose, which is to make your ideas happen. It's a passionate business and you have to be cool about it, or no one – except those who know your work and love you very much – will understand what you are trying to communicate. But if by trying to nail down and explain what you mean you lose the passion, you will lose the power that will ignite interest and attention in the idea.

An extraordinary and beautiful jacket can be made by ripping out the lining of an old but well made suit jacket, turning it inside out, and using the variety of colour and texture in the facings and paddings and thread to create an effect.

The solution to this equation will be different for everyone. Designers tend to have a visual response to the world. Moods have colours and texture, and the arc and pace of a narrative may, in their minds, be patterns, shapes, dimensions and weights of colour. It is as hard to reveal the way you picture a scene or a character, so clear and prominent in your head, as to explain why a phrase of music or poetry makes you cry. It can be as incomprehensible, when brought out into the light of a production meeting, as a being from another planet landing in the middle of the table. The key is to make it clear to everyone and to keep their confidence in your work without blurring the picture and the passion.

DRAWING

The first tool for doing this is drawing. Everyone draws as a child, and everyone who can see will understand what you mean from a drawing. Drawings also work as

A Meeting and its Repercussions

The director and designer have to set the parameters of a scene, with music but no words. It involves four giant puppet birds dancing in a field, which later turns into a river of puppet boats. They both know what they want to achieve in this scene and from this meeting.

The director wants to find a shape for the playing area that will allow the dynamic movement of the birds and a way to show the audience, without complicated instruction, how to clear enough space for the action. The action suggests the crossing of two diagonal paths, but there seems no natural reason within the story why this should be so.

The designer would like the audience, who will be standing or sitting in the field, to clear a space for both puppets and performers that will draw the focus to the visual drama of the scene; the audience will in effect become the walls of a stage full of the colour and movement of costumed actors and birds.

Both need to find a way to focus the attention to the right place in this vast space. The lighting designer would solve the problem if it were possible to use lighting, but the event will take place in the daytime.

THE PRACTICAL SOLUTION

The cross shape suggests to the designer the shape of a bird in flight with the tail to head and wing tip to wing tip creating two pathways and a central space. The outline of a bird in flight will be drawn on the grass the way a football pitch is marked with white paint. The audience will fill the outside curves beyond the white line to create the shape of the stage. Two 40m long lengths of blue fabric will appear, drawn by the bird animators to make a river for the boats to sail down.

FURTHER ACTION

These decisions will require action from other members of the team who will need clear information on what has been decided; production manager, stage manager, event manager, costume department, puppet makers, choreographer and performers will all be affected by the plan. They must:

* Get permission to paint the lines on the field
* Check the chemical content of the paint to make sure it is safe for grass and wildlife
* Check the regulations on fireproofing for the fabric river
* Source paint and painting equipment for the 40m bird
* Source fabric that will be light enough for performers to manipulate, and which can be bought with the budget allowed
* Ensure there is a dry space for the fabric river to be set so that it does not become wet and heavy if the weather is damp

reference points for ideas you want to talk about, and will help you to a logical explanation of your thoughts. These do not have to be carefully executed excellent designs or working drawings; they can come later if you need them, and can be created in the calm of the studio.

VISUAL STIMULI

Visual or tangible material which reflects the picture the stimuli led you to imagine, will help explain to the rest of the team what is in your head. It may be difficult to explain this with words and be sure that people understand what you mean, whereas images will clarify your words. Perhaps when you first heard about the project you thought of a particular range of colour: a picture, not necessarily of a character who might appear in the performance you are discussing, but one reflecting a visual aspect you want to make clear, the movement of a particular weight of cloth, images from film that may

* Make a working drawing with measurements of the bird shape to be drawn on the grass
* Work out some cheap and easy way to mark out the shape for rehearsal, as painting will only occur just before the dress rehearsal in the hope that it will only have to be done once
* Review the costumes of the bird animators and the puppets before deciding on the colour of the silks
* Check the schedule for the first rehearsal of the scene so that the mark-out of the bird will be in place
* Puppets, even if they are unfinished, should be available and strong enough to use for rehearsal; this sort of scene is difficult to rehearse without them and the fabric

The audience sits at the edge of the bird's wing. (Photo: Mark Griffin)

1 Rough sketches for the production; 2 samples and pieces of fabrics; 3 at work on the costume and puppets; 4 a young actor in costume awaits his entrance. (Photo: Mark Griffin)

not reference an appropriate time or place but are imbued with the weight of atmosphere that you imagine.

It can be helpful to create a series of very small pictures of the visual action you see in your head. These may be disconnected and reflect colour or atmosphere rather than narrative material, or might look rather like a comic strip storyboard. The fact that they are small, and a dozen can be taken in one eyeful, lends them a casual air, and stops yourself or others feeling tied down to a design at too early a stage; they merely hint at possibilities.

The era, place and style in which the stimuli lands the work may not be the same for all the creative team involved in a project, and it is necessary to be clear about the way you see it. A shadowed image of a man in a doorway wearing a trilby and wreathed in cigarette smoke will evoke the whole feeling of the style and era of 'Film Noir' in an instant. A Muji catalogue, a picture of a rider on a Harley Davidson motorbike, can create a visual vocabulary that can be understood quickly and clearly. An illustration from The Book of Hours will put in people's minds the ordered precision that may hide the inner life of the medieval church and court – or two

When dyeing, remember fabric changes colour when it dries.

Images that give a glimpse of the designer's thoughts.

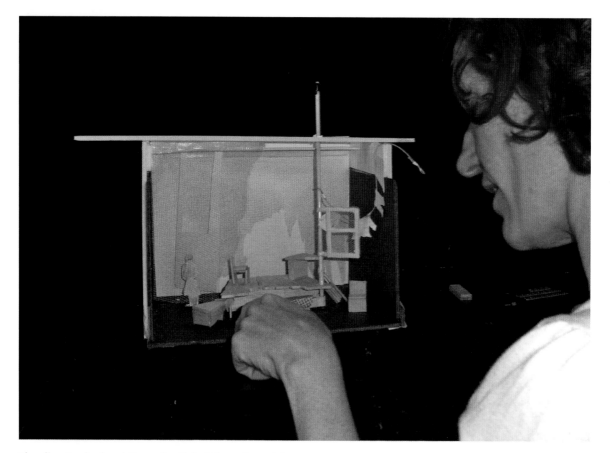

The director looks at the potential of the set model.

images, perhaps of a demure Victorian woman and the Amazon jungle, which when put together show a turmoil of two different worlds meeting in time and place.

SET MODEL

A rough model can be a great help to everyone as a three-dimensional way of looking at the world you want to create, and is the frame within which the audience will see the costumes. This is particularly relevant to devised physical work, as the use of different levels on stage opens extra possibilities for movement, making separate areas of time and place, and creating exciting stage pictures. The fact that there is something tangible to talk about, even if it is only a case of destroying every aspect of the structure, helps everyone to eventual understanding and agreement, and leads towards the settlement of the world the characters will inhabit.

The model will need to be more or less in scale, with a few figures or people-sized oblongs of card that can be moved around on its little stage. It is better if it has no sides if the meeting is likely to be a big one, so that everyone can see without clustering in front of it. It is an advantage to have some bits of cardboard and a pair of scissors, to be able to make instant changes in order to follow suggestions.

Wrapping paintbrushes and rollers in Clingfilm or polythene bags means you don't have to wash them between coats.

By the end of this meeting the model may be ready for the rubbish bin, but it may also have saved many hours of meeting time – even if not a single aspect presented in it is used in the production.

Playing to your Audience

It is essential to be careful when choosing the way to present ideas, and adjust them to circumstance. For example, it might be counter-productive to wave pieces of silk around at a meeting of a town council that you hope will sponsor your work, whereas you can wave and wind metres of fabric at a meeting of choreographer and dancers and they will understand exactly what you mean and probably play along with you. But you could make a drawing of your waving fabric and present it at the council meeting, and the mere fact that it is on a piece of paper on the table rather than waving in the air above their heads will make your thoughts accessible and acceptable to the members of the council.

COMMUNICATING WITH DIFFERENT PEOPLE

The Producer
A meeting with the producer may be the first time you can speak about your idea for a project, and the way you do it will affect the whole of its future. Most of these people have busy lives, and as far as they are concerned, your project will be one amongst many. They will be interested not only in the artistic nature of the work, but also in its more practical aspects, and whether it can be funded. Be prepared to discuss more than the creative possibilities. For example, possible venues for the performance will show a producer the scale you imagine, the sort of audience that you expect to interest and a rough idea of the budget that will be required to fund the work, as will suggestions for the number of performers and of the creative team, with examples of their previous work. Visual material, particularly of any research and development work around the subject, will help show the style of the work that you envisage.

It may seem strange for a designer, rather than a director or writer, to have to prepare for this sort of meeting, but contemporary devised and physical work muddles the disciplines together. Physical theatre direc-tors are as likely to be inspired by images or music as by narrative, and the designer can help to make these images concrete and clear.

The best outcome of this meeting is to confirm the possibility or probability of a production that will give you the opportunity to get your work seen by the public, and for the producer to have added an artistically rewarding, fundable performance or company to their credit. You are most likely to achieve this if you are clear and concise, and give the producer material they will find useful, and include a good dose of practicality with your inspiration.

The Director
Devised physical theatre tends to call for strong visual content, and the working relationship between director and designer in a devised show is close. Mutual under-standing and exchange of ideas, and the frank discussion of the work in progress, is the core of this relationship. The working method of this partnership begins early in the process, and its verbal and visual vocabulary will start with their first discussion of the style and content of the show. Both must have the same clear understanding of this, even if it is at an early stage of development, to create a firm base that will underpin the invention to come.

The way the design progresses has to be constant – the audience will eventually arrive and will have paid to see something when they do – however, the manner in which the design evolves will change with the working practice of each director. For some the presence of extra people in the rehearsal room when improvisation is in full swing is a hindrance to their, and their performers', invention of the work; in this case time must be built into the schedule in order for the designer to see what has been going on during the day, and to talk about it with the director. Others, despite the extra expense of time and space, like to have the designer and the whole creative team inventing by their side for as much of the time as possible, and the notes and sketches made during rehearsal will be worked on later or during short breaks in the course of the day.

Most directors hover between these two extremes, and a working practice will develop that gets the best result for both them and their designer. The way this

Three beds of light. (Photo: Nik Mackey)

develops will set a pattern for a working partnership which, if successful, may continue through many different projects.

Production, Stage and Technical Managers

There is an unfortunate balance in devised work, in which the performers and director push to keep changing and inventing to the last moment, whereas production, stage and technical managers need facts. These managers drive the practical side of a project – a particularly difficult job for a devised production, as so many concrete decisions happen late in the process. They have to manage the budget, the schedules and space and the company.

There may be a team of people doing these jobs, or one person doing all and a lot more besides, and the designer will liaise with them on many different levels. They are the people who need to know what money has been, or needs to be spent, and what is being bought with it. They can arrange times for meetings and fittings. They share with the designer the necessity for setting the balance between invention and concrete decision. It is possible, and indeed likely, that an improvised moment in rehearsal can set off a whole new direction to a scene,

and someone in this group of people will be responsible for gauging if it is practical to continue with its development.

These moments can occur right up to the last rehearsal. In a small team it may be impossible to have a stage manager in rehearsal all the time noting everything that happens, but the designer-in-rehearsal can help by communicating changes and new ideas as they occur to help keep everyone up to date with what is going on.

Funders

Funders are not likely to be interested in an extravagant and ill thought-out dream, though they will be interested in an artistic content that suits their policies. They look for clear angles. They want to know how to place a show, what content there might be in it that can be used to open a particular door, and what benefit, artistic and financial, it will give them. They will want to know if the show is financially viable, and to see that you have thought about the costs that might be incurred.

They will also question the public benefit of the work, the type of audience and venue, the experience and past record of the team you have on board. They will want to know if there is a demand for the work, and whether it

A very quick change will work best if it is choreographed and rehearsed like a dance.

has a purpose or direction beyond the artistic concept that might interest others in the project. If you can have a dialogue with them before you work on the presentation of your proposal it will help you to steer it in an appropriate direction.

The Performers

Meetings with performers, whether in a pre-arranged fitting or over a cup of coffee, are among the most important for a costume designer. Meetings about costume for physical performance are more complex than any. Like any other costume, the clothes have to look right and feel right, but for extreme physical work they must also allow bodies freedom of movement, and they must be safe. The skill of the designer is to understand and negotiate this balance without losing the quality of the design.

The only people who really know the way their bodies need to feel are the performers. They understand from the clothes they choose to wear for rehearsal, and the pain and inconvenience when they get it wrong, where they need extra padding to protect their knees from a trapeze bar or their thigh from a rope burn. Detailed discussion with the performer will prevent the carefully designed lines of a costume being cluttered, when it is actually being worn on stage, by such additions as kneepads or the webbing that trapeze artists use to improve their grip, which are out of keeping with the design but necessary to the health and safety of the performer.

This information might not be offered without prompting. Performers take their skill and much of the pain and danger of some of their work for granted, and attach small importance to it unless it goes wrong. Observation in rehearsal will help reveal questions that must be asked so that the designed costume is practical for the work.

The Musician or his Music

There is a link between visual design and music which goes deeper than the sound costumes can make, though in today's theatre that can also be relevant. The connection rests on the rhythm of moving bodies and fabric, and the way that light plays upon their surfaces. A meeting with a musician, unless it is definitely connected to the way a costume or set is used in a live soundscape, is more likely to be a meeting with music as the language rather than the words; the person does not have to be there, though it is good to talk if they are. The human reaction to sound waves and colour at the heart of this connection is as instinctive as moving to a beat, and as old as light. It is difficult to think of a military march as dove-blue silk chiffon, or a waltz as iron scaffolding – obvious examples, but that is the way it works.

4 Discovering the Style and Creating the Designs

How to use Stimuli and Research

The gathering and use of research related to the stimulus of the work forms the backbone of the development of a devised performance. The research for the design of costume and objects, and the research for the actual creation of those designs, have a different emphasis. The process that sets off the idea for creating a performance can start from many different sources, and the same source can be the catalyst for ideas to people with different interests.

The stimulus could stem from a written biography, history or political situation; for instance, a biography about the life of Byron could suggest to a writer a play about Byron and Shelley with Mary Shelley by Lake Geneva; to a director, a journey through Europe which follows Byron's life, work and loves; and to a designer, a comical shadow puppet play of his extraordinary coach journey over the alps. Myths, legends, fairy stories and folk tales are useful starting points, as they tend to address universal themes in a theatrical way. Characters such as Faust, Odysseus and Don Quixote come to life over and over again as hooks for a company for characters and ideas.

At his very first meeting with the designer, the director of the work will use references to other pieces of work or events to communicate his thoughts and plans for its style and content. The way these references are presented varies, but their purpose is to make sure that director and designer are heading in the same direction. Established director/designer partnerships will have a way of talking together which references past work or shared experience. New teams, without a past history of working together, must establish a language and a set of references, and these will develop during the work.

The choice of material to bring to an early meeting can be difficult for both parties. A director who has had the project milling around in their head for months or even years will have files of notes and references to books, poems and stories, music and images, which will have grown as the production nears its first day of rehearsal. The designer, as soon as they heard about the job, will have begun to collect or rough-sketch thoughts which might be useful later. An exchange of information and resources online may have happened before the actual meeting, and there may be a certain amount of shared information already in place. This first exchange is, nonetheless, most important to the life and growth of the relationship, and gives the designer all sorts of clues to the way the work and the partnership might develop.

COLLECTING IMAGES

The designer now has to make the collection of images that will grow into a strong and communicable concept. They will be images that apply to the mood, era and social stratum of the story, and the point of this stage of research is to make sure that the growing images all support the style. It is easy to go off at a tangent: ideas flow, but sometimes the exciting visions they produce may not give the audience the message you are trying to

St Mary's University College in *Klockwerk*. (Photo: Lisette Barlow)

Images that stimulate invention. (Photos: Alex Byrne)

The movement of skirts in rehearsal… and in performance. (Photo: Nik Mackey)

convey. Solid research makes sure that the tilted little hat with the alluring veil that is so apt for the character, belongs to the right era.

There is a balance between the way the designer wants the costume to look, and the movement it has to encourage. This balance is not too hard to achieve with modern clothes, most of which are designed for an active life. Period dress, both for men and women and particularly for the upper and middle classes, was designed for rigid and restricted movement, and for bodies that had developed the sort of muscles needed for that movement. This muscular development affected fashion then as it does now. Thus pictures of eighteenth- and nineteenth-century beauties show them with narrow shoulders, tiny waists and feet and big bottoms and thighs, while fashion images today show us broad-shouldered, slim-hipped and supple women.

In fact those earlier women needed strong thighs (hidden under their big skirts and petticoats) to support the apparent fragility and lack of freedom in their corseted upper bodies and narrow-backed dresses as demanded by fashion: try curtseying to the ground and floating up with grace in tight little shoes and a wheelbarrow's weight of skirts. Of course they couldn't run with all that cloth flapping round their legs. The long supple muscles, strong shoulders and throats fashionable today give a different strength to the contemporary physical performer, and it would be counterproductive to design for them an accurate period costume.

Points of View

During this development, more research sources will appear. Others in the team, including the director, will be working as you are. They will be thinking about the research and stimuli from different viewpoints; musicians, lighting designers and, above all to a costume designer, the director and whoever is responsible for the choreographic content of the piece, will be creating their own ideas based on the same body of research and discussion. More information will arrive as the project progresses.

The texture and variety of colours within a golden range give the light a chance to show what it can do. (Photo: Lisette Barlow)

The designer's viewpoint will always be based on what the audience watching the work actually sees, and what they understand from the visual elements of the work. Audiences may not all be skilled at recognizing the finer points of cutting or costume history, but they understand the messages that design gives, and are particularly good at decoding costume. All children use the dressing-up box to help their imaginative life, and the skills they develop so early still exist in adults, though they may not be conscious that the same skill is used by the costume designer. An audience may be better than a designer at the adaptations one must make when creating costume for physical performance, since they do not have the worries and doubts about the correct

Prepare a repair kit of patching scraps and mending items for a touring company to take with them.

application of period research, or the exacting details that tell of status or age. They may not appreciate the reasons for the dozens of social messages given by the colour of a handkerchief and the way it is placed in the top pocket of a man's suit, but they will understand the messages it gives.

The style of movement, even at this early stage of development, must underlie all the costume designer's work because if the design and movement are not working in tandem, the costumes, however perfect when static, will fail in performance. Consider a woman's legs and the extremes of angles in which they can move, and then think of the hundreds of different ways that skirts have covered them over time, from the eight-metre hem width of the nineteenth century to the pencil skirt of the 1950s typist. Neither helps the dancer or acrobat, and in fact both would prevent them doing their best work.

The costume designer has to accept these unwelcome strictures to their invention, and think of some way to give the audience an impression of the style in clothes that are practical. Establishing this through shared research and discussion with whoever is responsible for the movement, must be included in the baseline of the design concept.

THE COLOUR AND TEXTURE PALETTE

The audience, as well as the designer, holds the key to understanding the messages given by the designer through the costumes, set and lighting. There is no single reason for the choice of colour and texture that form the basis of the design for a production: instinct and a sort of cultural understanding work with the stimuli and research to create a palette from which the designs will grow.

Some of these are straightforward; if the place where the action happens is drawn from reality, a colour and texture range which has been informed by an understanding of that region will influence the palette. A realistic play which happens in a rural, agricultural past will call for rough linens and wools in colours that reflect the earth and land of the area; this might put forward a picture full of greens and browns in a country with a climate such as in Britain, but would be better served by umbers, creams and ochres in Spain, or white and blue-grey in the Arctic. Put the story in Victorian London, and grey and black, and dark purples and maroons start to creep in.

The mood, always so dependent on the light which floods it, is particularly influenced by colour: thus dark colours tend to create a sombre mood, and brighter tones a more cheerful one. This in fact oversimplifies a complicated and subtle psychological effect, because like music, light works to alter the way people react to a situation. It is obvious how music affects the emotions and the physique: bodies, eyes, stillness or movement and a sort of emotional alertness make this perfectly clear. If you doubt the way light plays the same tricks on emotions and bodies, just remember how people will smile, relax and open out their shoulders in sunshine, but how easy it is to fear and imagine the worst in the dark. Spooks vanish in light, and angels light up darkness.

The colours and textures in which the designer chooses to dress the cast give the light a surface to work on. Different surfaces reflect in different ways. Some, like white satin, reflect the light, and others, like black rough wool, absorb it. Muted colours can contain a wide variety of possibilities because they react so generously to different colours and strengths of light. For example a pale grey cloth can be lit in many different ways, particularly if, in the make-up of its colour, it contains subtle touches of red, blue and yellow. In an open white light it will look almost white, but with a steel gel colouring the light it will look silver; a red gel over the light will turn it blood red, and blue will send it into a moonlit night. And if there is a fair proportion of red or yellow in the make-up of the grey dye it may be turned to a rustic brown.

A red light on a red cloak will make it glow as if it is lit from within, whilst a green light will turn it to a brownish dullness. Beige and the lighter browns can be lit to look like gold if a golden light enhances a yellow pigment in the dye. These colour changes can be checked in the workroom or shop with one of the useful little books of colour gels which are given away free by lighting firms and a simple paint chart from a DIY shop. Best of all is to have a stage light and a collection of gels in your workroom so that you can check what happens to colours under different lighting, and can talk about it with the lighting designer.

Mood and movement in an abstract world. (Photo: Nik Mackey)

Movement attracts the eye, and a moving fabric will make a bigger patch of colour than a still one. Draw round the area that is covered by the cloth of a circular-cut skirt as the actress wearing it whirls around, and then do the same with the area covered by a straight-cut skirt, and you will be made aware of just how much difference cut and movement can make to the size of the image the audience will see.

The movement involved in physical theatre helps the designer. She does not have to rely on nature's wind to create the air movement that will make fabric flutter and flow, as each movement will change the way the fabric of the costumes hangs. Costumes must be designed, cut and fitted to let this happen – unless they are planned and made as hard-edged blocks of colour and shape.

The grouping of colour in a space offers another way of creating large blocks of colour effects. Again this is a matter of not confusing the image. A block of performers in different shades of blue will have more impact than one where several colours are mixed together. Some colours are more sympathetic to each other – for instance some reds and yellow can work well together in the same impact, whereas others, perhaps where the red has a tendency towards orange and the yellow a tendency towards green, will lessen each other's impact. Black is uncompromising and definite, and is invaluable when used for accents and stresses.

The society and social situation is another pointer. Beautifully woven, expensively patterned fabric, flurries of lace and decorative ruffles have no place in the

A lead pencil scribbled on an obstinate zip will lubricate it.

ploughed field unless to contrast the aristocracy with the harsher world of the worker. The audience, unless they are very close, will not be able to see the quality of cloth and weave – but they *will* see the way that light reacts on the surfaces, and how the cloth hangs on the body and the way it moves in the air, and they will be quite expert enough to translate the messages this gives them into a relatively accurate understanding of the social situation of the wearer. Even a very young child will choose glossy satin for a princess, dull rags for a beggar, or shiny silver for a robot.

GENRE

The genre of the piece puts another aspect into the designer's view of colour and texture. In many dance pieces, particularly in contemporary dance, and for other types of physical work, this can be an over-riding factor. The place and characters can be so abstract as to give no factual information to the designer's concept. In this case the style of the movement, and the music and sound that accompanies the work, gives more concrete information about the people on the stage, and about the place where the audience must imagine them to be. Instinct, and an understanding of the way colour, texture and light affect the audience, will lead the process that helps the world the choreographer is making on stage pass across the footlights to the audience.

The best way to understand this world is to sit in rehearsal and watch. Talk will help, as will sharing the choreographer's research and previous work, and listening to the music – but nothing will help as much as watching and listening with an open imagination and noting what tumbles into your head. Then you can watch some more, mentally dressing the performers in your imagined costumes and seeing if they fit with the movement and the mood.

The Designs

Most contemporary physical performance is devised. There is an exchange between director/choreographer and performer that continues throughout rehearsal, and one feeds off another. An improvisation may suggest a performer walking through the air on the upturned hands of the rest of the company. This needs precise rehearsal to actually happen, and no one may know until strength and skill have developed further, whether it is actually possible. If it is, perhaps it will be incorporated into the narrative; if not, another movement series that gives the same sort of feeling may be invented. Both may give the designer different ideas for the costume design.

Rather than presenting a finished set of designs, the designer may find it more successful to offer rough sketched suggestions instead of finished drawings, and may be conscious that some of these imagined costumes may have to include features that are not yet thought of and may have to be made in a rush. It is rare to get to the first night of a physical theatre performance and not want to re-cut all the costumes from the start using the knowledge you have acquired during the invention of the piece.

THE BALANCE OF TIME, BUDGET AND EFFECT

The amount of money available to spend on a show plays a significant part in the way the designer decides to fashion it. Allocating the way this money is spent is particularly difficult when making a devised show, as there is no way of knowing how the performance will develop. The unalterable facts are that unexpected expenses will occur, plans will change, and the money never seems enough. The way you use your budget must allow for these changes.

The safest way is to set aside a contingency sum of at least a quarter. If your budget is tiny this may be eaten up during a dress rehearsal by replacing a pair of broken shoelaces and a metre or two of cloth to replace a pair of trousers that ripped at the tech. The contingency money of a more generous budget might pay for the cloth, haberdashery and the maker's fee, and enable you to redesign a costume at the last moment because there is an idea for a new sequence.

The start of the rehearsal process, and the last few days before the first night, will be the most expensive. An approximate rule is that you can expect to spend about a quarter to a third of your budget on things that will never be seen in performance. To director, designer and actor it will seem that many items of costume or props, and possibly scenery and effects, are absolutely essential to the work. However, many companies need to experiment with these items before they can realize what really will be used in performance, and what will be discarded. This may seem wasteful of both time and money, but it is a necessary part of the process. The skill of the designer and the shopper lies in finding items that are representative enough of a costume or object to play with constructively, and to be able to place an accurate guess as to when that item has become embedded enough in the performance to warrant spending time and money on buying or making the real thing.

Many of the inventive companies creating devised physical work are young, and engaged in a constant struggle for funds. The budget for the whole show may be so small that it can be difficult to set aside a specific sum for costume or props. It is, however, impossible to create a practical concept which can be made for the performers to wear and the audience to see unless you know how much money you can spend.

It is not helpful to be asked to spend as little as you can: if the budget is small you will do that anyway. People who do not have the experience of making may not realize that a large roll of thread, a packet of machine needles and a couple of metres of elastic can cost as much as a day's food. Cloth is often the least expensive part of a costume, particularly when the quality of the stitching thread, strengthening tape and interlinings may be of vital importance to the safety of the wearer.

Shoes eat up a budget. The shoes that may be safe to wear on a dance floor will ruin actors' feet during the run of a performance that takes place on concrete, as their knees can be jolted to injury through the lack of protection provided by an unpadded insole. Dancers and physical performers know the type of shoes that are suitable for their work, and although it may be expensive to invest in shoes that combine their knowledge with your eye for design, it must nevertheless be considered.

Underwear and protective padding may have to be included in your budget, as in many cases it will be altered or stitched to the costume. Body protection against friction burns, pressure and grip is essential on some circus equipment, and your design must protect the thighs and arms of the girl on the Chinese pole with a hidden leotard or the feet of the man on the tightwire with the right shoes. The audience may never notice some of these hidden charges on your budget, but they all have to be paid for.

All these, and other strictures to your design, must be absorbed as certainly as any other form of research, or your ideas will be blocked all the time by their implacability. Once they are in place you are free, and can forget the negative aspects of their demands and allow yourself to imagine and make the world you want to see happen on stage. It is important not to let lack of money clog up your ideas or the truth of your design. There is almost always a way to make the feeling you want to give the actors and the audience, even though it may not be the way you first thought of, and may have to be found in a recycling bin and not in a shop. If you are clear about why you need to use a particular colour, texture or object, you will be able to find a way to create that effect. Objects do not have to be real to give the illusion of reality to an audience.

BUDGETING TIME

The time it will take to make the designed costumes is a matter of consideration for any genre of theatre production. Devised work adds an extra element. The invention of the performance continues right through the rehearsal period, and often beyond, and the costume designs must have a built-in ability to absorb these changes. The way you see a character at the beginning of rehearsal may be very different to the way that the actor and director develop that role in the weeks of improvisation and invention that follow.

The research into the genre and the setting of the concept before the designs are created will have set firm ideas about style and practicality. The designer for a devised piece of work has to come up with a way of dressing the performers that uses all this research and allows for the widest possibility of change at the last moment.

A basic costume for each performer, which reflects the place, era and genre as well as the character, is the safest way to allow these changes to happen. A costume that

The back of a spoon is a good tool for stretching shoes when using leather expander.

Characters in basic costume change their natures with added shawls. (Photos: Lisette Barlow)

Establishing the Genre

A performance is envisaged that takes place in several cars. Each car has a driver/performer, and an actor and two members of the public. The cars go on different journeys which start and finish at the same point. There will be many twenty-minute journeys throughout each evening for each car, and timed tickets are sold for each journey/performance. Though the performance takes place in London, the director wants the people in the car to feel as if they are in Paris in the 1960s, and that as soon as they get into the car they have become part of a louche and glamorous world.

The director brings to the meeting images of the cars, of casually elegant women in smoky bars, and of Paris streets under the streetlights. He also has a script of the dialogue and action that will take place during each journey, and a cast list of characters that will have a part in the story. He has references on his laptop of clips from films and music that give the feeling he wants to create.

The designer, whose only information so far has been that the show will take place in cars driving round London in the 1960s, and that it has a strong physical theatre element, has a very sketchy idea of what is needed and goes to the meeting armed with a sharp pencil and an open mind. She also takes a few images of film stills or fashion shots that show the costume, make-up and hairstyles of the time. At this point neither director nor designer have any shared vision of the way the design will develop – it is all in their separate heads. The purpose of the meeting is to join the two visions so that they can grow.

As the director begins to explain his ideas, using the images as a starting point, the growth begins. The designer can imagine the smell of the beige leather upholstery of the car, and feel the drama as it jolts to a halt in a cobbled courtyard: the chauffeur jerks open the door, and the audience sees through the car window a choreographed fight between the chauffeur and a policeman. The policeman's cape and hat are silhouetted against the street light, and it becomes clear that he must be dressed in the iconic gendarme uniform in order to demonstrate that we are in France. The actress in the car playing a mysterious woman must be dressed in a rich and vibrant colour to contrast with the dark of the chauffeur's suit and the gendarme's uniform.

The images the director has with him now become part of the shared knowledge, and can be used, in combination with the designer's sketchbook, to pin-point the way the design will develop, and form the basis for further research into the style and era of the story.

Other thoughts and questions crop up and are shared. The fight is in effect a dance, and to throw yourself around the street and wrestle on the bonnet of a car is difficult in a cape and hat; thus although the costume must be designed to look like a gendarme from the audience's point of view, it must nevertheless feel free and unconstricting on the dancer's body.

Should the chauffeur be in uniform, or in a suit and tie? Should he wear a hat? What shoes will he wear that will look right with his uniform, but not damage the expensive paint finish of the car as he throws himself around on it? Will the mysterious woman get out of the car, and if so, should she have a coat? A bag? A hat? The designer shows an image of both a fox fur and a trench coat, because the director's response to the images will help further clarify the way he wants the audience to feel about her – although another sort of coat may be chosen after the designer has worked on more detailed and appropriate research.

does not allow for alteration and addition will put the designer in the position of having to block moments of invention because of the impossibility of re-making the costume in time. Basic costume does not have to be uniform: each actor's basic costume in a production may be different, but they will all share the ability to be transformed by the addition or subtraction of detail and styling without a major re-make of the shape.

The solutions you come up with to navigate problems of time and budget may become a positive help to your invention, as they will force you to look for different ways to achieve the effects you envisage. The freedom to

The handwritten text within the image reads:

THE LAST GOODBYE

Husband in tweed or poss
pale grey with black polo neck
broques silk scarf

Matching dress
& coat
black
accessories

Coat & dress clth more day than
cocktail.

The Lady in Red.

A coat and dress designed for the type of movement envisaged by the choreographer.

invent during rehearsal can apply to the costume designer as well as the performers, as long as the preparation has been apt and the design concept allows for change. The images you create to show others the way you are thinking must reveal their openness to change and development, and help you, as well as everyone else, to see their possibilities as well as their established facts.

The creative team will meet to pool thoughts and visions sparked by the stimuli they have all been given, and share the research they have done on their own. The images you show will join with their ideas to create the basic fabric of the show.

5 Design in Rehearsal

The best option for any devised performance is to have the whole creative team in rehearsal for most of the time. However, this is also expensive, and many budgets cannot afford all their weekly salaries throughout the rehearsal period, and have to compromise by paying the designer a fee for the job. In that case it is up to you and the producer to decide how much time you can afford to spend in rehearsal. It can become a financial necessity to work on several jobs at the same time, and share out your rehearsal time accordingly. It is important to be clear and open about this when you accept the job, as no one except yourself and your team know how much time is used out of sight in preparation, designing, shopping for and making the show.

Unplanned visits to rehearsals may show the designer nothing more visually stimulating than the whole company near the end of discussing an idea. It is helpful if a routine is set in place so that all the creative team has an opportunity to see how the work is growing. A weekly showing of the state of play saves time being used up in arranging and attending production meetings. Sound, lighting, set, costume and object designers and makers can join the company, see and discuss the developments, and keep the whole group within the loop of the work.

Designing in Advance

It may be that a set of costumes has to be designed in advance of the first rehearsal of a devised work, as they would be for a scripted play. These can only work as base costumes for the performers, and will be added to later.

Ockham's Razor in *Every Action*. (Photo: Nik Mackey)

If the parameters of time and money make it necessary for the designer to work before, and away from, rehearsals, they must accept that the costumes the audience will eventually see may be very different from the ones envisaged, and must design accordingly. They will have less control over the synchronization of design in the costumes, props and objects that appear on stage. The clarity of the original idea may vanish beneath the undesigned additions and alterations that have been included during rehearsal to support the development of the action.

It can be possible to retain the integrity of the design by deciding with the director and the company in the pre-production stage that any additions will have a connection to the original design. The invention of the improvising performers will be limited to the costumes and objects you have chosen for them to use in rehearsal; their improvisation will come from the way they wear and use your selected clothes and objects.

Imagine that the original stimulus, from which you must design the work, is a story about an Edwardian vicar's daughter who eventually, through a series of as yet unscripted trials, triumphs and tribulations, becomes a tightrope walker in a circus. You know in advance that the costume of the company will have to change from the formality of Edwardian dress in the vicarage world to the gaudy theatricality of the early twentieth-century circus world, and that the objects used in the story will have to adapt in the same way. You can set in advance the costume designs. If it is in your brief you can pre-design the objects, from teacups to caravan steps that you imagine might be needed. What you cannot do, without severely limiting the invention of the improvisation, is keep a designer's eye on the additions and alterations that become necessary to invention.

Making stand-in props in rehearsal.

A more abstract stimulus may enable you to design a basic costume, together with a collection of accessories and objects that you are happy to see together on stage. The colour palette will be limited to the shades you have chosen, the textures will be apt and the objects will suggest reality rather than be real. The actors may have a pile of hats, scarves, coats and skirts designed to fit a large range of sizes to add to their basic costume. They may have a heap of sticks, pipes, string, lengths of fabric, containers and other non-specific objects. In addition to this, the designer will need a small tool kit of scissors, sewing kit, saw, glue, tape, elastic, wire, pliers, gaffer tape (duck tape), safety pins and cable ties.

It is possible, though difficult, if you have set all these visual suggestions in place, to allow for design improvisation by people who cannot see through your eyes, and still keep the visual message you hope to deliver from becoming muddled. When you revisit rehearsals you are bound to be shocked by the way the scene you see in front of you differs from the one in your imagination, but it will not be as far from your concept as it would have been without the limitations you have set in place. It may be relatively quick and easy to rescue your original pictures without upsetting the way the work has developed.

Designing in Rehearsal

When working on a devised, physically demanding show, the best situation is for the designer/maker to be free to spend as much time as possible in the same space as the work develops. The most perfect state is for the workroom, with its drawing and cutting tables and workbenches for relatively quiet work, to be in, or to adjoin, the room where the director and performers are inventing. When this happens the design and the making of the show can feed each other and grow together.

Many performers who work in this field have at some time had to sort out their own costumes and props, and are good at the sawing and sewing and sticking that goes with costume and puppet making. Their knowledge, especially of a particular technique or piece of

Cover surfaces and tables if you are gluing or painting in rehearsal, particularly if there is a dance floor.

TRANGA & her MUSOs.

Tranga in tail coat with pockets – pass painted face and little horns under hat all in yellow with Yellow/black dyed chef's trousers or hams.

A basic costume of yellow trousers and T-shirts is added to from a collection of appropriate accessories and props.

equipment, can prove invaluable. The designer cannot tell in advance that a planned and rehearsed fall will hurt in a particular place – but the performer with the bruises knows, and they also know the placing and thickness of the padding that saved their shin. You may imagine their costume to have a short skirt, but the lightness of the effect might be spoilt if the leg beneath it were lumpy with padding. If you are on hand you will be able to

Suggestions for Workshop Props

Sticks	Good for sound, for marking levels, for bodging puppets, and for weapons	Bamboo is light and comes in different lengths and thickness. Broomsticks or dowel is stouter though more expensive. Willow withies, or whips as they are often called, are whippy and bendable
Sheets or lengths of cloth	For flapping, wrapping, making walls and water and tables. For hiding and revealing	Ex-hotel stock is cheap. Cotton or lycra or other stretch white cloth is best to work with. White or black is most useful to the imagination
Umbrellas	Useful because they transform from a small neat shape to a large canopy and back again with ease, and they make good sounds	It is not worth buying expensive ones as they are bound to get broken – better to buy lots of cheap ones
Hats	Provide hats as different as possible. To wear, to balance on bamboos, to exchange and to throw	Try to source hats that suggest a variety of characters; there's no need to suggest an appropriate period at this stage

design together some smaller gaiters that look delicate and slim, and conceal padding beneath their soft leather.

DEVISING A THEATRE WORKSHOP

The process of devising a theatre workshop frequently occurs when casting and creating a company, and as a way of bonding and setting a genre for cast and crew. The designer has a double role in these workshops: one is to watch the way the company plays with the objects they have provided; the other is to focus on the style the

company will work in, and to begin to understand the way they must use their bodies in the costumes. Any costumes or props the designer provides for these early stages must be open enough to stimulate, but not lead, the performer's improvisation.

WORK ON A SPECIFIC STORY

Objects and costumes for improvisation round a specific story may need to be more specific to time, place and event. Exactly what you select to offer the company

A collection of objects that suggest a story or era.

Further Suggestions for Workshop Props

Seaside	Beach towels, a length of deckchair cloth, sunglasses and sunhats. Bucket and spade, bucket of sand, flippers for comedy!	To help set the outdoor feeling of holiday
Victorian	Top hats and bonnets, long skirts and men's suit jackets or blazers, walking sticks, corsets, formal shoes not trainers	To help set the quality of the movement affected by clothes of the time
School	Hats, caps, baseball caps, hair bands appropriate to the period. School uniform items, and a bag of rulers, cigarettes, exercise books, crisps and chewing gum, paper and bike bell, mobile phone and catapult	To give a collection of possibilities to play with that are appropriate to the era and the story
War	Sticks for weapons – broomstick-size dowel will stand in for most weapons (20cm gun, knives, etc; 60cm rifles, swords, etc; 110cm bows, staves, etc.). Hoodies and pull-on hats. Strong belts, scarves and shawls (women, babies, refugees). Drum	To help with creating the different characters and effects of war

depends on time and budget. For instance the weapons you offer could be the broadsword and dagger of the twelfth century, the bow and arrow of the Tudor archer, or the AK-47 machine gun of today's warfare – and sticks can represent all of them. It is much better to use a stick and imagination than a lightweight toy or replica, which looks like a real gun but feels wrong.

WATCHING THE WAY THINGS MOVE

A choreographer or movement director will see the work they are making as a sort of pattern reflecting the stimulus. Within this structure there will be sections that are clear and preordained, and others that are little more than a strong feeling for a particular piece of music, an idea, or a thought that will grow through rehearsal. The designer coming into one of these rehearsals will have discussed the idea for the work, and will have worked through any stimulus or research suggested by the director. However, unless they have had experience of working with the choreographer on other projects, the style of dance and method of working will not be known.

The first visits to rehearsal will reveal the type of movement and what the dancers look like as people; they, after all, will be wearing the costumes. Even today, ballet dancers, however individual they may seem to each other and to the more informed members of the audience, seem to look very alike to an average audience member, and the make-up and hairstyles, particularly for women, encourage this uniformity. Contemporary dance bodies, on the other hand, are much more varied: apart from their height, weight and age, the variety in their faces and colouring is a chosen and useful factor in the casting for each particular project.

This variety of choice is also given to the designer. Costume for the ballet world is still often limited by a traditional style which displays the clarity and perfection of the body's lines; ballet shoe and costume makers are extremely skilled at creating these traditional styles, and usually specialize in that single and demanding discipline. It is unlikely, in that world, to find a designer who is also a maker. The same is not always true in contemporary dance, where the making of costumes, and often the shopping for high street styles that can be adapted, form the greater part of the costume designer's work.

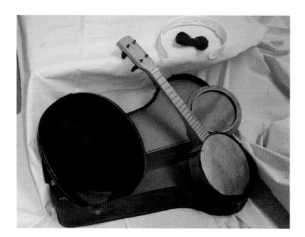 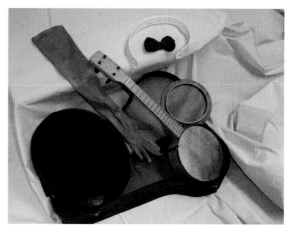

The emotional message of a group of objects is changed by the addition of a glove.

Some choreographers or movement directors work on performance that crosses the boundaries between theatre and dance. In these productions the costume may look like real clothes, as real as any naturalistic costumes in a period or modern play. Of course they cannot be real, and will have to be adapted to allow for the movements that must be performed in them. The designer sees what they should look like, the shopper finds the item or chooses garments that fit or can be adapted to the purpose, and the maker alters them to make them work in the action. One person performs these three jobs if that is all that the budget can pay for.

IMPROVISING COSTUME WITH THE ACTORS

It is possible, if it proves useful to the director and performers, for the designer to improvise alongside the actors by offering stand-in costume or props that follow and help develop the story paths the players have chosen. It may also be possible to change the path by offering a surprise: imagine what would happen if you took away a bottle standing in for wine, and replaced it with something that suggested a knife or a piglet or a bunch of orchids!

The whole balance and story of the improvisation would change. People are used to music working like this, and the power that music has to change the direction, pace and emotion of a scene is often used to spur on invention. You only have to watch what happens to physical performers when they hear a tango rhythm, or a soundscape of far-away shipping, to see how they are accustomed to using music and sounds as stimuli.

It is possible to do the same thing with objects, and it can have as strong an effect when it works. Nevertheless you have to know the direction the work is taking, and you must have an open and easy relationship with the director and performers for this direct contact to be successful. If it does work, it can integrate the design into the heart of the work, and give little discrepancy in the end product between the design you want to create, and the design the performers and director want to work with.

The designer will have to have assembled a heap of costumes or objects that apply to the world of the story. The improvisation begins and the designer, instead of noting an idea that is suggested by it and waiting to talk about it afterwards, can take something from the heap that will help the development of the idea as it grows, and offer it to an actor. Neither they, nor you, need to speak or acknowledge your offer, nor do they have to accept the item if they do not want to. You can remove,

Do not forget to allow for appropriate warm underwear and insoles when designing for outdoor winter rehearsal.

St Joan grows in rehearsal. 1 Early experiment with prop and costume. 2 St Joan watches the action on stage. 3 St Joan sets off on her horse to battle. (Photos: Alex Byrne for Theatre Mummpitz)

replace or offer anything without holding up the action. Something as simple as putting a red hat on one performer can change his state in the play from a minor to a major position.

Perhaps an improvisation that is flagging through a bleak moment of invention can be rescued and set off in a new direction by drawing a chalk line on the floor which divides the performers into two camps, or by placing a basket of oranges in a corner and waiting for someone to discover it and use it as they want.

It sounds chaotic and disruptive. The idea of walking on to a stage in the middle of an improvisation and changing the look of what's happening, not as an actor but as an outside eye, is an odd one, and not the way designers usually work. But it takes a remarkably short time to become an invisible and helpful producer of invention, and to be accepted by the company as being as invisible as a light or a piece of music. You will benefit by trying out the ideas and seeing what you need to do to make them suitable for the eventual performance.

You will see immediately what works and what does not work. Lengthy discussions and dead-end scenarios are kept to a minimum. A glance from the director will tell you of a direction in which she would like the improvisation to proceed, and you can offer objects that will suggest that path. A different sort of glance will tell you not to interfere.

The other most useful benefit to the designer in the devising process is that the performers and director can see the way they are thinking, and that you are a close and active participant in the process. They will trust both you and your ideas.

'The Masque of the Red Death'

Punchdrunk is a site-specific immersive theatre company, and for this production their venue is enormous. The performance will take place in its many rooms, corridors and cubbyholes, and its three theatre venues. The director and choreographer cannot be in all the spaces at once, and work daily with the dancers and actors to create a style. The performers then work separately or in small groups around the space, only meeting for big set pieces where the whole company works together in more traditionally choreographed moments.

The audience enters the building, each member is given a cloak and a mask, and they can then wander as they like through a past world while dramatic events unravel around them. The people they see on their journey become part of this parallel reality. The performers have been cast in roles inspired by the characters in Edgar Allen Poe's stories, but although they, and all the company, know their character, stories and points of interaction, the way these will be interpreted remains to be invented throughout rehearsal.

The costume designer's job in this work is to create – together with the set designers and dressers, scenic artists, and sound and lighting designers – an evening where the audience and the performers are immersed in another time and place, where the rules that usually govern their understanding of a situation are replaced by music, dance, sound and atmosphere. It is also to help inspire the performers in their invention.

It is impossible to pre-design a set of costumes for this work, and any attempt to do so would set a limit

The Masque of the Red Death, a Punchdrunk and BAC production, 2007. (Photos: Stephen Dobbie)

on the action. The designer must work in the same way as the director and choreographer, and will have to set a general style, design the set-piece company moments, and concoct the rest at the same time as everyone else. This can be inspirational for the performers, and they can play a big part in designing their own costume if the possibilities are set up with care. It is equally inspirational for the designer and makers, who can watch improvisations at any point, and produce and incorporate ideas, adaptations or radical alterations that will strengthen or facilitate the action.

The designer researches the period and collects a big stockpile of clothes, fabric, feathers and braid, hats and accessories: from fabric to fan, everything is appropriate to the time and period. The colours, textures and garments all lie within the range of style she and the director envisage for the characters, and they will work together for the scenes where the company perform together in one of the larger spaces.

The actors arrive one by one in the costume room for formal fittings and discussions, when one or more rough ideas for their costumes are settled, and confirmed with the director. The costume department works quickly to make these ideas practical for rehearsal, and the performers then go away and improvise with the ideas in their heads and on their bodies. As the scenes and the movement develop they return for more discussion and adaptation.

The whole process, though held within the strong frame of the director's original concept and research, is an intensely collaborative process.

6 Shopping and Sourcing

Shopping plays a major part in the design and creation of costume for devised performance. This may well be divided into two parts. The first will be sourcing, shopping for, and possibly bodging together in a rough and ready way the costumes that can be used in rehearsal for the inventing process. They will be chosen, of course, for their connection to the way the piece will play, but they will also be picked for adaptability of size and character suggestion. It may be that a full skirt with an elastic waistband is used in rehearsal as a skirt on a man, but also as a cloak, a flag, a dog and a funeral pall. None of these items may make it past the experimental stage to the actual show, but they will give the actors, the director and you, the designer, a chance to imagine the way a more finished version of the garments would look and feel like.

The fabrics used to make costumes for use in a scripted, naturalistic performance are usually designed first, and shopped for afterwards; the designer imagines and draws the costume, and the fabrics or ready-made items are bought according to the design. If the budget for fabrics is generous this will still be possible, but it is not always the most successful method when the costumes are going to have to withstand the stress, stretch and sweat that extreme physical action creates, and when the budget limits your choice of fabrics.

It can prove a more affordable and practical approach to begin to build a collection of fabrics that you know are right in colour, texture and behaviour for the performance, and to use this collection to form the basis of all the costume design work. These fabrics, when

Jonathan Lunn Dance Company in *Self Assembly*. (Photo: Nik Mackey)

spread out on the table, will show a straightforward view of the palette of colours and textures already in place, and the gaps in this palette will become clear as you allocate the various items to specific characters and scenes. It may also help to draw your designs in outline and only add the colour when you have actually purchased the fabric or clothes.

The advantage of using this method becomes obvious when you do not have enough money to bring to reality the ideas in your head. It may be that you have access to a stock of costumes, or have leftover fabrics or costumes from another show. Perhaps a few lucky finds in charity shops or car boot sales have given you cheap items that will fill in the gaps. Drawings which illustrate both where the gaps are, and the colours and textures already in use, can be carried around when shopping. Where budget necessity means that many of the performers will wear their own clothes, they will understand from your incomplete images what is missing, and will see what they may have or could borrow that could complete the costume you have imagined for them.

Choosing the Fabric

To start with, the fabric has to be strong, and if it is not strong enough it may have to be backed with a tougher fabric. This is not always satisfactory because a double layer costs twice as much and takes longer to cut, fit, sew and wash. It means more insulation for the performer's body, and consequently more heat, more sweat and more weight. If you have to back cloth, try to restrict the double layer to areas where you really need it, and wherever possible leave fabric unbacked.

To get this right you have to imagine the performer working in the garment, and note where the stress and

Trousers cut high to protect the performer from the winding and binding rope as she propellors to the ground. (Photo: Nik Mackey)

wear will occur. The best way to understand this is to watch a rehearsal of the action; the second best way is to ask the performer to describe and re-play the action for you at a fitting. The worst possible way is to make it and hope it will work because that is the way you want it to look, and then despair because it rips at the first dress rehearsal on an uncomfortable actor.

The choice of fabrics for this type of costume is limited when you do not have much money to spend. Many of the cheaper fabrics designed for dance are brash and visually vibrant, and bear little relation to the everyday wear of the man in the street or the non-chemical colour

range of period costume fabric. Many of the yarns that are used in stretchy fabrics have a shine that reacts strongly to stage lighting. This may be useful for some styles of performance, but the circus/showgirl look cannot be taken seriously when the performers are working on stage in what is supposed to feel to the audience like an office or the Sahara desert, even though they may be working on identical equipment.

Sourcing the Fabric

The first step for the design of the costume, once the initial discussion and research has taken place, may be to wander round the fabric shops and markets that suit the budget. Go armed with a pair of scissors, a stapler and a pen and paper. Some fabric shops limit the number of samples they will give, particularly if they are situated anywhere near a college where design students always want samples of cloth for their portfolios – although once they know that you are a serious shopper they may be more obliging. If not, you can sometimes offer a small sum of money to allow you to take a lot of samples. If the worst comes to the worst, and you really want to have a sample of the cloth to consider, test dye or show, you will have to buy the smallest quantity they will sell you: in some cases this will be 10cm, in others half a metre.

Once you see a fabric you think might be useful and that you can afford to use, unroll a metre or so to consider it as a possibility; a shop or stall that does not let you do this is no good to you. Look at the way the fabric hangs when hanging down straight from the roll, and when you dangle it from one corner. Look at the way it behaves when you wave it or blow it, and feel its weight as it hangs from your hand or when you put your hand underneath it and hold its weight like a little table holding up a tablecloth. Test its stretch: down the length and across the width, and its crosswise or bias stretch. Feel its texture, and notice how smooth or rough it is when it moves over your skin, whether it slides over easily or sticks.

Note whether the light shines on the fabric (like satin)

Keep a pocket full of cash – markets don't take cards and interns sent shopping might be broke.

Buying a garment for its cloth may be the best way of sourcing an elusive fabric.

or sinks into it (like rough linen). Note the composition of the fabric and whether it will wash or have to be dry cleaned. If its texture, behaviour and price are good, but the colour is not, consider the possibilities of the dye pot – a fabric of impossible brashness may be toned down if it has only a 20 per cent content of some dyable fibre mixed in its strident tones. Then ask for a sample, or if you are certain, buy it; it may not be there next time you shop, by which time it might have become a mainstay of your fabric collection for the show.

Shopping for the Dye Pot

You may be lucky enough to be working on shows where there is a dye room, with experts on hand to match fabric and clothes to your pictures. If so you will probably not need this book. It is, however, more likely that you or your helpers will have to do their own dyeing at home or in the studio, with ordinary domestic equipment. Whichever is the case, the use of dye to make otherwise incompatible fabrics blend or contrast, look aged or brightly new, is a force to be reckoned with.

Some fabrics are difficult to dye without specialist equipment. Natural fabrics such as cotton, linen, wool and silk dye easily, as do man-made fabrics made from natural products, such as viscose, which is made from wood. Some fabrics may shrink in very hot water, though this can give an excellent effect of rugged thickness if you need it. Polyester will only retain the ghost of a bright colour in the dye pot. Luckily for the designer of dance and circus wear, many of the stretch fabrics such as elastane, lycra and suchlike mixes of yarns take dye readily.

It is always worth testing a sample if you have doubts about the composition and dye-fast capability of a fabric: you cannot always believe the labels, particularly if you are buying cheaply in markets or economy fabric shops. You can usually tell from dipping a scrap into a jam-jar of dye of any shade what is likely to happen when you dye a whole length of cloth, and after a while, experience will give you an instinct for what will dye and what will not. The instructions on the packaging will give you a good idea of the colour and fabric types under ideal circumstances. It is often possible to obtain excellent results in a much more rough and ready way by heating

If you think you may dye a costume in the future, use cotton thread to sew it; polyester thread will not dye.

colour mixes in a large old saucepan and dipping in scraps until you have the shade you want.

Shop-bought clothes have a label stating the composition of the fabric of which they are made. This may be difficult to find, and not stitched into the back of the garment along with the maker's name, but hidden in an inside seam. It does not usually state the sort of thread used for the stitching, and it is likely that the thread on a cotton garment will be polyester and so not take the dye in the same way that the actual fabric of the garment does. Nonetheless the label is worth looking for.

The present colour of the garment will also make a difference to success in the dye pot. A yellow cotton shirt can be dyed to a darker yellow, or a brown, a green or a red that is orangey rather than mauve, or interesting shades of grey or beige. This is because all these colours have yellow in their pigments. But if you try to dye the yellow shirt purple it will be a muddy purple, as the yellow will muddle the purity of the colour. A blue shirt, however, would dye to a rich purple, as the blue would enhance the depth of blue within the purple. The technical explanation for this is illustrated in the colour wheel; however, if you are shopping for cloth to dye, it is probably simpler to remember that the colours of the rainbow next to each other will be sympathetic to their neighbours in the spectrum, and go from there. Alternatively imagine the colours you would use from the paintbox to mix the colour you want.

The way a fabric is woven and the yarn used in its manufacture are the factors responsible for its strength and stretchiness. It is a common mistake to make stitching stronger than the fabric it holds together. Any stitching should only be as strong as the cloth, and if you doubt its suitability for the job, buy half a metre of cloth, stitch two handles on it very strongly, and get two people to tug each end: if the fabric tears then your stitching is stronger than the cloth, and you cannot alter that fact without using a backing fabric; but if the stitching comes undone you can stitch more strongly with tougher thread.

Many lightweight, man-made yarns are strong and have an inherent elasticity that is particularly useful.

How the colour of light and dye affects other colours.

Powernet, which is a fine, elastic net, and some lightweight lycra mixes are extremely light and strong. Also some fine, light, natural yarns, most particularly silk, have a strength that it is hard to believe from their fragile and diaphanous appearance.

Testing the Stretch of a Fabric

To test the stretch of a fabric, first lay a ruler or tape measure on the table, then lay the fabric on it and hold it down to the table at the start of the measure. Pinch it between thumb and forefinger at the 20cm mark and stretch it along the ruler and see where you get to. Do this across the fabric, down the length and across the bias, and each time note whether it springs back to the original 20cm mark when you let go. If you are in a shop and this is not a practical proposition, stretch the cloth over your fist and between your fingers to get a rough idea of how it will behave when worn.

Shopping for Garments

There are two sorts of costume shopping: one is a search for particular items and possibilities, and the other is a sort of trawl for ideas. The first requires you to note down what you see and where you saw it, to check it is available in the size you want or can alter to fit, and to find

It is worth using button or extra-strong thread for sewing fastenings, etc., as it is quicker and stronger.

out if it will be available when you need to buy it. If you can photograph it, so much the better. The second is more a search for the items that you definitely want to see on stage, and then to make sure that you can afford them. Both sorts of shopping can be done in reality or on line. It is essential, if you buy an item, to get a receipt and to find out the company's policy for returning or exchanging goods. Note the latest date for returns, as it is easy, in the rush close to the date of the opening performance, to forget that the items may have to be paid for even though you end up not using them.

Many of the bodysuits, tights and so on that form the basis for extreme physical performance costume will not be returnable once the packaging has been opened, and taking accurate measurements of the cast will help to make sure that money is not wasted in this way. It is helpful to ask the artists if there is a particular make of dancewear that they know will fit them, and which works well for their particular discipline. Most will know if they usually buy small, medium, large or extra large, and they will also know of recurring problems in the fit of garments. For example, some may find that the shoulders are too narrow, or the body length or sleeves too short or too long. Nevertheless it may be more reliable to alter and build round tried and tested favourites, than to risk buying something that does not work on the actor's body even though the sizing information appears to correspond with their measurements.

INTERNET SHOPPING

Shopping on the internet gives the costume shopper a huge range of choices without having to trawl round shops. If you know what you want, and can trust the supplier to deliver the correct items in the time scale they promise, it is quick, easy and very efficient. If you are not sure what you want it can be a long-winded, frustrating process and leave you biting your nails as the delivery time passes, the dress rehearsal gets nearer and nothing has arrived. And of course you don't really know what the item looks like or feels like until you have it in your hands. Colours as shown on a company's web site may be inaccurate, and the sea summer blue you imagined may arrive as a harsh turquoise. Sizing can vary with companies and manufacturers; a size fourteen or a size ten dress may fit an actress better than the size twelve she usually wears. If the item is wrong or not suitable you cannot nip back to the shop and change it – once again you must rely on the efficiency of their delivery method to right the problem.

It works best to find what you want on a company's website, then get the contact details and ring them. You can then talk to someone who knows the stock, and can

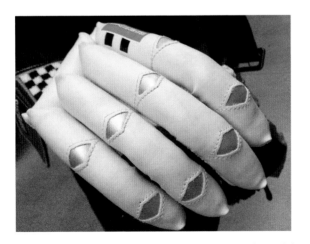 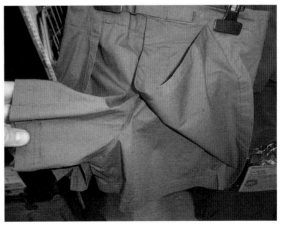

Clothes designed for specific sports can be adapted for costume use.

Have a place where you always put receipts.

Car Boot Sales and the Like

Car boot sales, jumble sales and markets offer more than bargains to the designer and maker: they present a varied and unstructured collection which could never be matched by a shop. You need to be strict with yourself to get the best result from this sort of shopping. Opportunities for design and invention will lure you at every turn and you will see things all the time that you feel you might never find again. A rusty and ravishing birdcage hints at a story you haven't heard yet; a dustbin bag spilling ruffles of cotton petticoats into the mud will present an opportunity you can hardly bear to miss.

But if you are shopping for one show with its time and budget in mind, you must narrow your focus, avoid these temptations and shop for the list in your hand. Force yourself to see only the colours, textures and particular objects you need that day. Clothes and fabric get buried in heaps and boxes, but with practice you can tell which stalls are likely to have clothes of the style and period you need by spotting books, or a chair or a pudding basin from the same era, country or class. Once you have mastered the knack of this filtering process, the stuff you are looking for will attract your interest in sharp focus and the rest will blur into a background of muddled colour and shape.

The other use of such a jumble of colour and texture is to search for ideas. It may be that you are trying to

think of an object that will be used in improvisation to stimulate stories of long-ago childhood; perhaps you find a battered musical box that can still just produce a tune, or the patriotic costume worn by a child for a victory street party on Armistice Day. Who could resist the shine of silver leather tap shoes or the texture of cream wool pre-war vests to add to their workroom store for future productions? The exposed cogs and levers in a broken metronome case, with its rich colours of polished wood and dark gleaming brass could set the base of colour and texture that will form the basis of the design of a production.

Take bags that are easy to carry, and lots of change, and remember to write down the prices for your accounts, because if you ask for a receipt you will cause mayhem or mockery.

An old metronome mechanism sets the tone of a production.

ask what you need to know. If the person you talk to is well informed and helpful, try to get their name so that you can get back to them later or ask for the same person another time. Once you have discovered a web site which is accurate in their descriptions, reliable in their delivery and reasonable in their prices, you will use them over and over again.

Paying for items bought on line can be problematic when working for a small company. There may not be a company credit card you can use for Internet purchases, and your only option might be to use your own and reclaim the money afterwards. Make sure you have included VAT and delivery charges in your estimate of the cost of your purchases. Also be clear about the delivery address and whether there will be someone there to receive the package. It is frustrating and time-wasting for a parcel to arrive when there is no one to receive it, and to have to re-arrange the delivery for another time. When working away from home, the receipt for the items may automatically be sent to your home address, so there will be a delay on you being able to re-coup your money from the company. Ask for a receipt to be e-mailed to you. It is worth checking if the company you are working for has accounts with suppliers that are useful to the show, as they may be able to claim a discount.

Shopping for Costumes

Of course the choice available to you depends where you live or work. Even where choice is limited you will have favourite shops, which will tend to have the sort of stuff you like to use. At some point, in a show that involves a lot of movement you will need to find somewhere that sells dancewear. If you shop in any big city this is not difficult. In smaller towns you may have to resort to the sort of shop that sells clothing for dance classes or the local school-wear supplier. They may not have everything you need, but if internet shopping is not an option, they may

be able to order more quickly than you can, and may even order several sizes for you to choose from when you can see them.

It happens, when a show calls for contemporary street wear, that you will shop in the high street for everyday clothes that you can adapt for the extraordinary demands that may be made of them on stage. If you are well organized it can be good to take the performers shopping with you, and though both you and the shop personnel may be white-haired by the end of the day, you will know the clothes fit and feel right for the movement.

The other option is to go prepared to carry a great deal and get a variety of possibilities in different sizes, which you can fit and return as necessary. This type of shopping needs preparation and steely self control. You must know what you are looking for, and not be sidetracked. This is easy when shopping for someone else's designs as you are trying to re-create the pictures they have made, and are not in the position to make choices outside that brief without consultation. When you are shopping for your own ideas it is more difficult. There are always compromises to be made, and it is easy to spot a garment towards the end of your shopping that would have affected the previous choices you have made throughout the whole process. You have to decide if you have time to start shopping again, and whether the new design ideas set off by your discovery are so valuable they cannot be ignored, or whether calm reflection will reveal the new thoughts as a whim which will never be noticed by the audience.

It is of immense value to a designer to work with a good shopper. It is not an easy job, and to find someone who has the skill, understanding and observational powers to work to the pictures, colours and textures that are invented by someone else is a godsend. They are as valuable as good cutters and makers, and have as great a part in creating the costume that is worn on stage. The job is not given the status it deserves.

7 Cutting for Movement

The weight of an overcoat or jacket can be reduced by removing fabrics that don't show. (Photo: Nik Mackey)

It does not work to design the same clothes for highly physical movement as you would for naturalistic acting. The result may look the same to an audience, but such clothes cannot feel the same to the wearer, and will cause endless trouble if the quality and vigour of movement have not been thought about in the design. Costumes have to allow for extremes of mobility, and the shape of the clothes is dictated by these extremes.

St Mary's University College in *Nights at the Circus*. (Photo: Lisette Barlow)

Changes in Body Measurement during Movement

There are dramatic changes in body measurement during movement. The expansion of the nape-of-neck to heel measurement when the actor is standing and when he is touching his toes will be many centimetres. Similarly a tensed bicep and a relaxed one may be very different if the muscle has been developed for strength. This alteration in length and breadth has to be allowed for when cutting costumes, and disguised by the shape of the garment and the stretch inherent in the fabric and design.

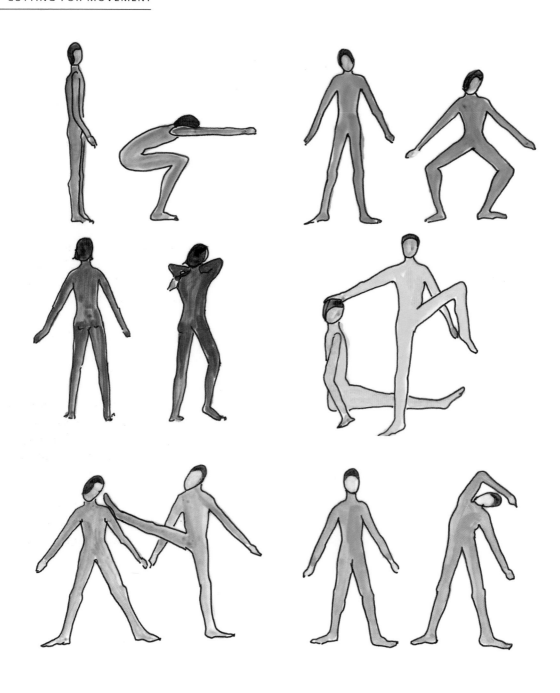

Allow for certain measurements to alter during movement; these would include: a) nape to ground, both straight and arched; b) waist to ankle, straight and bent; c) across the shoulders relaxed, and the arms crossed in front; d) waist to ankle, knee straight and flexed; e) inside leg seam with raised leg; f) underarm with the arm over the head.

For example, if an actor stands and raises his bent knee to his chest, either the trouser leg must be wide enough to slide up his leg, or the fabric must be stretchy enough to expand the extra inches that his bent knee demands. If the cloth is stretchy enough to do this it must either slide back to the ankle when he lowers his knee, or it must not matter if it sticks in wrinkles over his calf and behind his knee. If neither of these allowances is made either the cloth will split, or the actor will be unable to lift his knee, and a new pair of trousers will have to be designed and made. Similar allowances and variations of design must be made for all areas of the body.

The wonderful improvements in stretch fibres have made this problem much easier for both actors and designer today than it was for our dancing and acrobatic forbears in their knitted tights and bathing suits.

The weight of the costume is another consideration and will affect the design to a certain extent, although its overriding importance comes when shopping for cloth. A performer will sometimes be able to use and enjoy working against the weight of a costume, particularly if they are playing a character older than themselves. It is, however, much more likely that the jacket which looks so structured and solid on stage has had its linings, interlinings and stiffenings removed, or is made more lightly and has more flexibility than a costume for a production where more naturalistic movement is used.

It is much easier to use a stretch fabric to make costumes for extreme physical movement, but there are occasions when you cannot incorporate that sort of cloth into the design. In such cases you will have to resort to other strategies to allow people to move freely and safely in their costumes.

To understand quite how much the measurements of bodies change in movement, stand up and be conscious of the way your body feels. Stretch one arm, with the elbow bent, over your head close to your ear to reach your other ear. You can feel with your other hand how much difference there is in the waist to armpit measurement of the stretched side before and after the movement. Bend sideways and feel how much more is added to the measurement. You have to allow for these, and other differences in the cutting, buying and altering

of costume, and you have to see the performer moving at a fitting to make sure you have done it right.

Fitting Trousers

The most likely problems with trousers will occur because they slip down over the hips, which creates restriction in the spread of the crotch. This can be made worse if the calf of the trousers is too narrow to slip up the leg, which makes it difficult for the knee to bend.

Men, women and children have very differently shaped bottoms. There is less difference between hip and waist measurements in men and children, than in women; also in women the curve of the hip is softer and more pronounced than in men. Women are more likely to have a convex curve between their hipbones, and men a flatter one. Women's trousers need a more pronounced curve at the side-top to allow for and fit to the curve between the hips and the waist.

CUTTING OR BUYING

When cutting, remember that the curves and angles of bottoms and legs are beautiful and expressive parts of the body, and cut to make the most of their long or curving lines. If you cannot make doubles of costumes that are going to lead a hard, sweaty life at the beginning of a run, keep an accurate pattern.

Changing the relative lengths of rise and leg is a useful way of altering the look of the body's proportions. Think of traditional clown trousers, with their over-shortened leg length and up-to-the-chest rise.

Do not skimp on length when cutting trousers: it is easy to take them up and make them shorter, but much more difficult to add to them.

When cutting it can save a metre of cloth if you add a piece to enable you to cut the back crotch section; this means you can cut the trousers 'head to tail' and place the pattern economically.

Cut trousers high enough to sit neatly at the natural waist, or cut them so that the cloth rises above the waist and use braces to keep them up (this is particularly beneficial if extra protection is needed over the back or belly). Trousers designed to be worn below the waist with a low crotch must be baggy enough to allow for a full sideways leg stretch and upward kick.

The extra high-cut trousers which protect the back from equipment…

…are hidden from the audience by a waistcoat. (Photo: Nik Mackey)

Very stretchy jeans are available, if you search, which people can do the splits in. You may need to reinforce the crotch and centre back seams and to alter the waistband so that it does not bag at the back waist over the spine on an athletic body.

Look for men's trousers that are cut with a high rise (the length from crotch to waist) for period productions.

Narrow trousers with a downward stretch can be worn with braces and an instep strap for a smooth line, as long as the fabric will stretch enough to cope with an up-to-the-chest leg bend.

Cut the calf wide enough to allow the trousers to slip up the leg over the calf muscle if you want the trousers to slide back to a straight position after a bent knee movement. Note that the size of this muscle changes by several centimetres when tensed or relaxed.

Set the trouser length when the leg is straight, and check it again when the leg is bent, when the length is much shorter. The trousers may seem worryingly long, and consequently sloppy and dangerous, to a performer, but it is worth reminding them that it is possible that the action, which requires a bare section of ankle, may only occur when the leg is bent.

When cutting or buying for a man with a large stomach, make sure the front seam is longer than usual. If the actor is very large the front seam may be longer than the back one.

When fitting the waist of the trousers, make sure they are set at the correct height at the crotch, and then mark the height of the front and back at the natural waist. Unless these two points are in the correct place, the trousers can never hang perfectly on the body.

Fabric conditioner can make fabric slippery and unsafe on trapezes, etc.

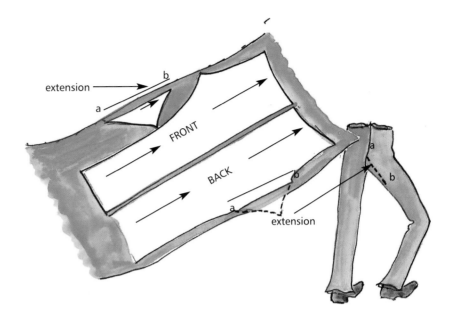

Save cloth by cutting the crotch section separately.

Consider, where appropriate, the simple traditional pattern of Thai fishermen's trousers, dhotis, Kung Fu trousers and the like, which have been developed over centuries for ease of making and fitting and movement potential.

ALTERING TROUSERS

* Add a high-stretch waistband to non-stretch trousers.
* Avoid pockets in narrow trousers if you can, so as to give a smooth hip line. Remove and sew up unnecessary pockets for a smoother line.
* Check that fastenings are strong enough. If the fastening placket is longer than necessary, sew it up as far as is practicable. Buttons are the safest fastening, with a button or strong trouser hook at the top. If one button goes it is not a disaster – if a zip breaks, it is.
* When performers have to use their ankles to hang from equipment, climb ropes or silks, or to provide hand- and foot-holds for others, it may be necessary to cut trousers shorter than you would like. It is worth leaving enough spare at the hem to work out the maximum safe length for the performer in that particular production, as a problem encountered in one show may not occur in the next.
* Wide-cut trousers will slip up the leg when the actor is upside down. You can restrict this slip if you need to by attaching a ring of soft elastic to the inside leg seam at knee level. If this makes the trousers hang weirdly, add a flap of a few centimetres of tape to the seam and attach the elastic to that.
* If friction burns on the legs are an issue, it may be necessary for the actor to wear flesh tights under trousers to protect their skin.
* Insert or stitch a section of elastic into the back waistband to stop the trousers slipping.

Skirts and the Pants Under Them

The ever-present problem with skirts and physical theatre is pants. Underpants must pass unnoticed unless you intend the audience to see them. Other likely problems are a restriction of the leg movements caused by skirts with too tight a hem, skirts falling over the face, or a gap appearing between the top of the pants and the waistband when the wearer is upside down. Period skirts can be too heavy because of the amount of cloth needed to make them convincing. Performers should have practice skirts if the real thing is not available for rehearsal.

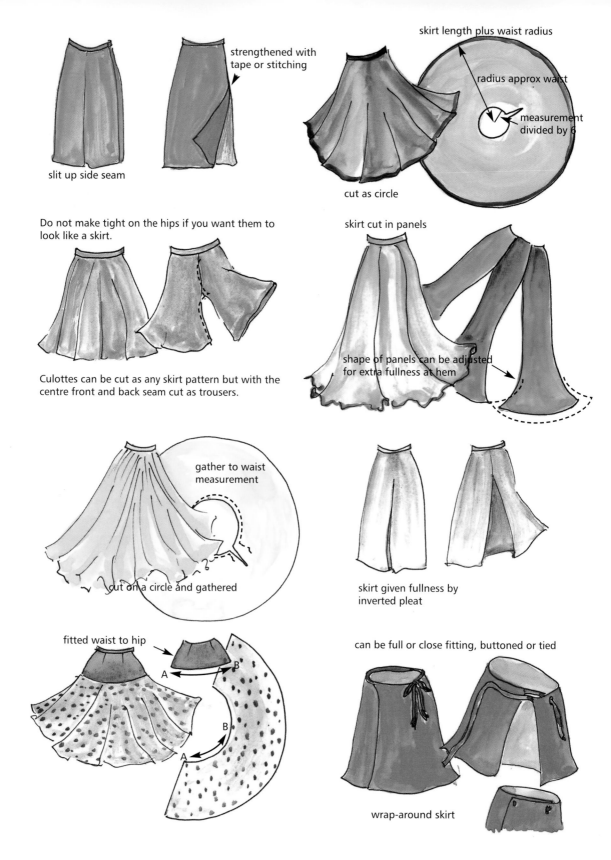

slit up side seam

strengthened with tape or stitching

skirt length plus waist radius

radius approx waist

measurement divided by 6

cut as circle

Do not make tight on the hips if you want them to look like a skirt.

skirt cut in panels

Culottes can be cut as any skirt pattern but with the centre front and back seam cut as trousers.

shape of panels can be adjusted for extra fullness at hem

gather to waist measurement

cut on a circle and gathered

skirt given fullness by inverted pleat

fitted waist to hip

A

B'

B

A

can be full or close fitting, buttoned or tied

wrap-around skirt

Skirts well adapted to movement.

CUTTING OR BUYING

Skirts give a designer the opportunity to use the colour and drape of fabric for effect. Very few physical performers choose to rehearse in a skirt, unless it is a short stretch one worn over leggings or tights. This is a sure sign that skirts present difficulties in movement.

When choosing fabric for a long, full skirt, search carefully for a material that is light, even if it has to look heavy. It may be necessary to back a see-through fabric with an opaque one to get the density of colour and the lightness you need.

The lower part of the skirt must be wide enough to allow for the fullest stretch of leg allowed by the movement. A narrow skirt can be designed with slits or pleats at back, sides or front; pleats hang straight but allow fullness and movement. A wrap-around skirt, short or long, allows room for movement as long as the cloth slips against itself and does not cling.

Any skirt cut on a circle can be shaped slimly to the hips and will flare naturally to the hem. A full skirt will look slimmer at the waist and hips if it is cut in a circular shape before being gathered at the waist. A gored skirt cut in triangular panels will do the same, and can be fluted out to ruffle at the hem and give the impression of more fullness than there is in reality.

Waistbands should be strong but soft so they do not cut into the stomach on a forward bend. A bias-cut facing on the inside of the waistband makes an excellent top to a movement skirt but may need stay-stitching or a thin cord inserted at the edge so that it does not stretch with time. A high waistband should be cut in clinging stretch fabric so that it does not roll or cut into the diaphragm.

Culottes cut to begin their outward curve at hipbone level can look like a skirt and present far fewer problems. Soft fabrics with minimum shine are most likely to convince, although there will always be moments in the movement when the audience can see that the skirt is really trousers.

An outward pleat, front and back, each side of the centre seam and meeting in the centre can disguise the inside leg seam completely in a short skirt, and partially in a long one.

Shorts made with a front flap can give the impression of a skirt.

ALTERING SKIRTS

* The waistband should fit snugly, and if wide should shape to the curve of the body.
* Waistbands should not be so tight that they interrupt the shape of the silhouette by squashing it.
* Fastenings, side or back, should be as flat as possible. It is relatively safe to use a zip on a skirt which is not tight to keep a smooth line.
* It is sometimes possible to make a skirt hang in a more flattering way by lowering the waistband a centimetre or two at the front; wrinkles in the belly-button area will indicate that it is worth taking the trouble to unpick and re-stitch. The same is true of women's trousers.
* Attention to the hem length has a double importance for extreme physical work. The back of the knees are used for hanging and may need to be free of fabric. The hem on a long skirt must allow the toes to just show underneath it or the wearer will have to negotiate each step to avoid treading on it.
* It may be that a skirt can be longer at the back than the front if the design demands it, or have a train. If so, the performer should have the chance to practise with it, or with a stand-in skirt, both for their own benefit and for others who might tread on it.
* The fabric of circular-cut skirts may stretch and drop. Make the skirt with hanging loops, and leave it hanging up for a few days before marking the hemline.
* It is worth taking the trouble to unpick a waistband before altering the side seams if a flat, smooth finish is wanted. 20cm (8in) of elastic sewn into the back of the waistband will ensure a snug, comfortable fitting. This should not be used as a gathering, but more to allow a few centimetres of adjustment in wear.
* To prevent a skirt falling over the face when the wearer is upside down, the side seams of skirt and knickers can be caught together with a few small stitches, a strong bar of thread or a short length of tape. Make sure this does not alter the way the skirt hangs. Test whether you have the attachments in the right place by asking the performer to stand upside-down.

In some women the waist measurement varies

a tape 'bridge' stitched from skirt side seam to pants seam

a tape 'bridge' stitched from elastic round knee to inside leg seam

Ways of securing skirts to underwear. 1 A tape bridge stitched from the skirt side seam to the pants seam...2 ... and one stitched from elastic round the knee to the inside leg seam.

considerably according to their monthly cycle; if this is the case make sure you have allowed for adjustment with elastic or double fastenings.

Underpants

You may want to make, buy or dye pants to match, or use plain black or flesh coloured ones. Some performers prefer to wear their own briefs under their costume pants. Always check underpants from the pant-revealing eyeline of a small person in the front row of the audience.

CUTTING OR BUYING

If you need to make extra sure that pants remain modest, particularly important when working with children, the best cheap option is to use the boxer shorts made for little boys. They are cotton, can be dyed, and a ten-year-old size pair will be snug-fitting and comfortable on a small woman. If necessary the buttons can be removed and the flies sewn up.

Most performers prefer to wear cotton underwear.

Specialist dance briefs for women are good but expen-sive compared to high street underwear. Full briefs from chain stores are better than bikini-style briefs, though thongs can be good for certain roles when you want the buttocks to be revealed, or the back lines of the costume to be smooth.

Men's boxer shorts can show a line under the costume, and slip pants are often a better option.

Dance supports for men worn under tights, or close-fitting stretch trousers give a neat if rather unnatural line to male genitalia.

It is quick and easy to make a pair of shorts-style pants from any stretch cloth; if the cloth is stretchy enough there will be no need for waistband or leg elastic, and the line will be smooth.

In some cases where you are particularly anxious that no skin should show around the midriff on stretches and upside-down movements, a sleeveless body may be a good option. You can also make a lightweight stretch pair of shorts with a vest-type top, which you can cut away to suit the covering costume.

If you want pants to look more revealing than they are in reality, it cheats the audience's eye if the performer

Let clothes that are warm from drying or ironing cool before you fold them to avoid creasing.

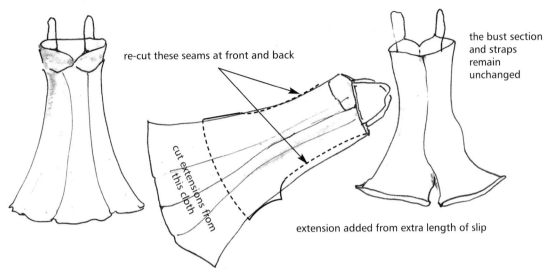

re-cut these seams at front and back

the bust section and straps remain unchanged

cut extensions from this cloth

extension added from extra length of slip

Making camiknickers from a standard slip.

wears a pair of skimpy pants or wide-legged French knickers over a flesh-coloured bodysuit, thong or pair of pants.

ALTERING UNDERPANTS

* The top halves of bought bodies or leotards can be cut away until they are little more that a pair of braces and high-cut pants.

* When sewing pants on to a blouse or shirt, work out the best position for a way into the garment. This may be an eccentric slit cut anywhere that can be disguised; it can be vertical, horizontal or diagonal, but choose the most inconspicuous place of the costume so that the wearer can wriggle in. It may be an opened shoulder seam or the centre of a side seam as an alternative to the more usual front or back fastenings. Most of the supple performers who need this sort of costume adaptation are adept wrigglers, so it may be that the opening can be much smaller than seems possible.

* Some fastenings get in the way of certain actions on equipment, and safety or comfort demands unusual fastening positions. It is usually better to position them on a soft part of the body rather than over a bone.

Shirts, Blouses and Bodices

CUTTING OR BUYING

Shirts and blouses can come untucked during any action that involves stretching the body. If shirts or blouses are to be tucked into a waistband they will need to be secured in some way in order to stay in place. Also make sure that the armpit-to-waist length is long enough to accommodate the stretched side seam.

If the sleeve is wide enough to move up the arm when the arm is above the head, there will be less trouble with shirts untucking. A cap sleeve on a blouse, which leaves the armpit free, will not restrict upward arm movement.

When buying shirts for physical work, make sure the shoulders are wide enough and the upper arms generously cut to allow for the strongly developed muscles of dancers and physical performers.

If you cut tight-fitting bodices at the start of the rehearsal period for work where performers are learning to use a new piece of equipment, allow enough in the turnings for alteration, particularly in the underarm seam, the sleeve and the centre back. It is surprising how quickly muscles alter in measurement during training.

Try to avoid boning as much as possible. If you do have to use it, make sure it is light, supple and washable and

stitching

elastic loops

sleeves slip to
allow upward
arm movement

sleeves re-cut to cap shape
to free arms

Blouses made or
adapted for movement.

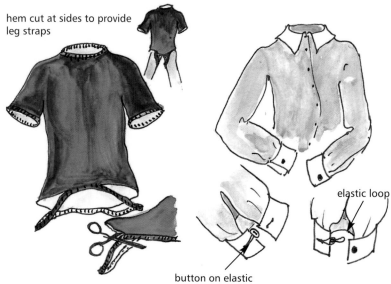

hem cut at sides to provide
leg straps

elastic loop

button on elastic

that the ends are carefully padded. Try to bone costumes so that the bones stop a couple of centimetres short of a natural fold of the skin. For instance, stop the bone just short of the waist seam or it will be uncomfortable on an extreme sideways bend.

A lightweight alternative is to 'bone' seams with strong twilled tape or Petersham ribbon sewn over the seam on each side. This will stiffen the seam slightly and discourage it from crinkling.

It is possible, on a slim body, to give the appearance of a boned bodice or corset by using a double layer of firm cloth. Be sure to pre-shrink this before fitting. A twilled weave – you can recognize this from the way the threads run diagonally in the weave, rather than horizontally or vertically – gives the firmest cloth.

A period bodice, or a bodice that you want to mould to the skin, is best cut on the cross of the fabric if you do not want to use a stretch fabric.

ALTERING SHIRTS, BLOUSES AND BODICES
* Attach the hem of the shirt to stretch pants to keep it in place.
* Add elastic straps to the bottom of the shirt which will hook round the thigh and prevent the hem riding up.
* Slits or an extra gusset in the armpit will allow more freedom of upward arm movements. A performer cannot lift their arms freely in a sleeved, tight bodice unless it has a slit under the arm. This can be incorporated into the design, or made as invisible as possible by backing the slit with a matching stretch net, or dyeing the armpit section of a blouse underneath it to match the bodice fabric.
* It will often be necessary to let out the cuffs of shirts and blouses so that they can slip up the arm more easily. The easiest way may be to add a small elastic loop to the buttonhole.
* A short-sleeved woman's blouse can be made free and more adaptable by cutting and facing small slits from the outer arm to the shoulder.

All-in-One Bodysuits, Bodies, Leotards, Animal Skins

The difference in measurement from the back of the neck, down the spine to the crotch changes by many centimetres when the actor stands straight or bends in a toe-touching crouch. This has to be allowed for when buying or cutting the garment, and there must be some way of making sure that a garment which is close- and neat-fitting on the body does not either pull or bind at the shoulders and crotch when the performer bends over, or produce a sagging bottom and wrinkled belly look when they stand straight. The stretch is most necessary above the waist at the back of the body, over the bottom, and over the kneecaps and elbows; you can get away with bagging above the waist if there is a tight, wide waistband below it.

The easiest way to allow for this is to use a stretch fabric, and to cut with the stretch running from top to bottom; two-way stretch fabrics make the cutting even easier, and fabrics have now been developed which stretch in all directions. Do not feel that you have to cut all sections of the garment with the stretch running the same way: it may be better for movement to cut the bodice in sections, giving the shoulder-strap pieces a downward stretch and adjoining sections across the back and chest a horizontal stretch.

CUTTING OR BUYING
Make or buy tights, leggings or trousers to be worn under a leotard of matching fabric to give the appearance of an all-in-one body suit.

If tights are being worn for warmth or protection the best option may be to buy cheap chain-store tights and accept the fact that they are a running expense and will have to be replaced for every performance.

Make sure the centre back crotch seam is cut generously, and cut sleeves wide enough so that they will slip up the arms if the cloth is not particularly stretchy. Cut trouser legs wide enough so that they will slip up the leg when the knee is fully flexed if the cloth does not stretch.

When making animal costumes (known as skins) it is a help to extend the centre front and back seams so that the crotch will be low and allow for crouching movement.

ALTERING ALL-IN-ONE BODYSUITS
* It is possible to inset a pointed oval-shaped gusset of extra fabric at the back of the waist as long as it can be disguised with some decoration on the garment.
* Insert elastic round the neck so that the neckline can

Opera dei la luna 2004

Cow

black velvet
ears

pink velvet
muzzle &
udders.

silver speckled
fur.

leather spats
over gym
shoes.

5'
actor

actor.

velvet curls &
ears

velvet
white patches.

— cowskin
dungarees
with
integral
'hooves'

Above: Design for a cow
showing the position of
actors inside the
costume.
Left: The cow checks
sightlines and the
comfort of the head at a
fitting.

slip lower down the back when the character bends, and will return when they stand upright.

* Open the seams at the armpits to allow an upward stretch, so that the bodice does not ride up.
* An elastic gusset can be inserted at the shoulders, but take care that it doesn't make the neck too low at the front.
* An elastic V can be inserted at the centre back to allow more movement for the arms and shoulders.

Dresses

The problems that occur with dresses, apart from those that happen with any skirt used for movement, revolve around the fitting of the waist and the shoulder and armhole seams. Most of the same problems that can occur in blouses and skirts also apply to dresses.

CUTTING OR BUYING

It is better to buy a dress that is too big and alter it to fit a body that uses particular muscles, which a dress cut for everyday wear may not accommodate.

Sleeves, short or long, should be wide enough for the biceps and forearms. Also shoulder width and the armhole should be generous. Physical performers often develop a muscle just above their armpit at the back, which can easily make an armhole tight.

It may be best to cut the bodice of a dress in stretch cloth even if the rest of the dress does not stretch. An alternative is to cut the sections at the side body, both front and back, in stretch cloth and incorporate the difference into the design.

Culotte-type pants in a matching cloth can be made and stitched into the waist seam of a dress so there is no pants problem when the performer is upside-down; the wide-legged pants will fall down with the skirt and not be noticed. They may have to be attached to the inside seam at an upper side seam or front and back seam. This method can also limit the extent of the fall of the skirt of the dress over the performer's face.

Coats and Jackets

The main problem with jackets is that they tend to flap about when open, or restrict the movement of the shoul-

ders when they are buttoned. One of their many advantages is the number of pockets, tricks, slings and harness that can be fitted into them without dramatically altering their outward shape. A jacket that fits perfectly and is well cut will be much easier to work in than one less carefully shaped. It is easy to make a beautifully cut jacket look tatty or rough, but you can never make an ill-fitting one look good, no matter how expensive the cloth. Waistcoats are a more comfortable way of creating a formality without the difficulties involved in wearing a jacket.

Adjusting the fit of the jacket pattern...

... and fitting the head of the osprey. (Photo: Mark Griffin)

CUTTING OR BUYING

Choose jackets without too much padding or stiffening unless the performer can use the weight and stiffness for his role.

It is often better to make, rather than buy jackets and coats for physical performance because then you can build in the lightness and suppleness required, whilst making the coat look heavy; a patched and tattered coat made out of real wool and hessian will be heavy and unwashable, whilst the same effect can be produced with rough woven silk and dye and a few carefully placed pieces of interfacing around the pockets and collar.

The sides of the jacket can share the same seams as a close-fitting waistcoat or vest; this will allow only the front to move when unbuttoned, while the back stays close to the body.

Make sure the shoulders of a coat or jacket are wide enough for the actor's shoulders, which may be more developed than most, even when the rest of the body appears light and slight. Shoulder pads look dreadful when the shoulders inside them move a lot.

The most difficult bits of a jacket to make look right if you are an inexperienced tailor are the lapels and the collar. If you are in that situation, it is probably easier for you to buy a jacket and alter the other seams to fit the particular performer and role.

The slits (vents) at the sides or the back of a jacket allow the hem of the jacket to spread out when the wearer is sitting; this is, of course, very useful for physical performers for all sorts of other movements.

Collars can get in the way of ropes and equipment. When the actor is upside-down they may obscure quite a lot of his face from the audience. The neck of a physical performer is often very expressive and you do not want to obscure it more than you must.

It is difficult for a performer to work upside-down in a jacket, as it all starts to fall about their ears. It may have to be attached at the upper underarm side seams to a fitted and stable undergarment.

ALTERING COATS AND JACKETS

* It may be necessary to shorten jacket sleeves to clear the wrists for gripping equipment or other performers.
* Fastened, waisted jackets and coats may need slits or underarm gussets or extra width at the back of the shoulders if performers need to hang by their arms.
* Make sure a jacket can slip off easily if it has to be taken off in the course of on-stage action.
* Jacket linings are more visible on stage as they are revealed by movement, and their shine catches the light. Make sure they suit the character.
* Sew up pockets if there is a danger of them catching or hooking on equipment, and remove or change buttons.
* Once you have taken out the lining of a jacket you will be able to judge how much of the padding, stiffening and interlinings you can remove to make the jacket more supple. There is always a balance to be struck between removing too much and losing the structure and line of tailoring, and allowing for freedom of movement.
* It may be necessary to open the back or side seam of a coat to give the spread needed for leg movements.
* Opening the curved armhole seam at the armpit where the sleeve and jacket body meet will help to allow raised arm moves.
* It is easy to fit a harness into a jacket without it showing, though hard not to make it rise to a point at the place where it is clipped off to the rigging. The most usual plan is to cut a hole as near to the harness rigging point as possible, and disguise the hole as best you can.
* A strop can be sewn into a jacket through channels or loops of strong tape that lead it under the arms and round to the back of the neck.

Many performers, particularly on first nights, need to go to the toilet just before they go on stage. Make sure they know how long it will take them to get out of and into body suits, which take longer than separate costumes.

Charlotte Mooney
for Hang-On.

matching
underarm
gusset of stretch
cloth to
free arm.

light wool
jacket.

floating
skirts go
under skirt
as well as for
upside down.

Poss another layer
(Cardigan?) for last
entrance.

lycra
underbody

cut cut for bottom
layer of skirt

top dress

Jacket design with underarm gussets.

Applying Decoration to Stretch Costume

It can be difficult to paint, pin or sew elaborate and exact decoration on a stretch bodysuit, tights or a leotard because these must be stretched to the correct size before you start. Sometimes it is enough to work over cardboard or to stretch them to a measurement, but at other times you may need to be very accurate and precise. The following is an easy, clean method of making an exact model of a performer's body if you need to shape a skin-tight stretch suit in order to paint or sew on elaborate decoration.

The actor should be dressed in tight underwear and should be sitting or standing in the position you want for the final dummy.

Wrap them in clingfilm so that all the parts of the body (except, of course, nose and mouth) you need to use are covered, and nothing can stick to their skin, hair or clothes. If the position is uncomfortable you can cover all the less bendable parts first and do the bent joints later, so they are immobile for a shorter length of time.

Use short strips – about 15cm (6in) long is a useful average – of wide sticky tape to cover the clingfilm, and create cellophane 'skin'. The strips can be a bit longer for less detailed, flatter areas such as the chest or back, and may need to be a little shorter for complicated folds of the skin such as in the armpits or groin.

When the body is covered the actor will be immobilized, and you may have to lift them and lay them in different positions to get all round the body. Cut through the 'skin' with scissors, and do this in wide zigzags so that it is easy to match the edges when you reassemble the mould. You will have to cut in several different places to free the 'skin' from the body. The clingfilm will come away with the 'skin'.

Tape the cuts together, using the zigzags to get an exact match, then stuff the skin with newspaper, or anything else that is cheap and handy. You might have to cut more zigzag slits to get the stuffing in, but it is easy to tape these up afterwards.

You now have an exact dummy to dress in the bodysuit or leotard.

This is also a useful way of making body parts such as odd limbs and masks (keep the nose and mouth clear of clingfilm and/or tape), and also life-size puppets. It is remarkably quick, clean and easy, and does not use much skill or money.

For a more durable dummy, fill the mould with the sort of aerosol foam used for filling cracks and holes in walls. Try this out on an experimental foot or arm section, as it is surprising how much it expands, and it is important to leave room for it to do this, or it will distort your mould.

Making a mould of the body: 1) Wrapping the actor in Clingfilm. 2) Applying the sticky tape in short strips. 3) The actor still wrapped but with the head released. 4) Legs out and the chest area cut ready for release. 5) Freeing the final sections. 6) The sections working as puppets in ultra-violet light. (Photos: Christine Jarvis)

8 Fittings

The progress of a devised performance from first rehearsal to first night is not the same as that of a scripted piece, and nor is the progress of costume from conception to the final garments. The time scale is different and schedules have to be more elastic to cope with the invention that continues to change and add to sections of the work until the last possible moment. The designer and maker, along with the producer, director or stage management team, will have different time scales when they know that changes must stop. For many directors the later in the process this comes, the better.

The best way to make an accurate guess as to which moves and actions are set, and which may change, is to spend time in rehearsal. You can also tell from this which performers like to know exactly what their costume will be like, and how they will work with it in the creation of their character. Those who like to be sure and use costume as part of their role-building process will benefit greatly from a costume that is finished early enough for them to wear in rehearsal until it is as familiar to them as their training clothes. Others prefer to work in their own clothes and only put on their costumes for fittings and practical trials; they use the lift and feeling of being a different person that costume gives them to add energy to their performance.

It is lucky for the designer/maker if there is a mixture of both types of performer in a large cast, as they will then be able to schedule their time more reliably. They will be more likely to make an accurate assessment of which costumes can be finished in every detail, and

Ockham's Razor in *Every Action*. (Photo: Nik Mackey)

which must be left with a possibility of change until later.

Active Fittings

Costumes for physical work must move with the performers. For them to do this you have to see the performers moving in the clothes, and making the movements that are used during the show. The way the maker and designer arrange fittings depends on the level of complication presented by the movement, the stage equipment and the rigging. Actors in naturalistic performance do not use each other's bodies with the same freedom as those in physical theatre or dance, and it is quite easy to fit them without seeing the work they are doing on stage. Hamlet and Laertes can show you the leg/arm stretches of their fight in the fitting room without having to wield the actual foil, but an aerial performer, suspended upside-down from a swinging trapeze holding another by her hands and wrists, cannot.

Physical theatre performers and dancers treat each other's bodies with the unconcerned lack of distance of young children in a playground. They use each other as climbing frames and swings, and the close contact called for by lifts and moves keeps them easy and familiar with each other's bodies and skin. This amount of actual contact between costumed performers presents particular problems with costumes and cloth, because often you are not fitting one actor, you are fitting the actor in the situation of being lifted by, or sitting or standing on, another and so you may need both for the fitting.

Imagine a move where a girl climbs on to the shoulder of a man, using his bent knee, hip and cocked elbow as a handy upward staircase and his head or neck as a newel

The movement and inventive possibilities inspired by this skirt could not be imagined from a description or mock-up costume. Left: The princess arrives… Below: …and her baby is born. (Photos: Lisette Barlow)

Puppeteers squeeze together to try on a patient horse. (Photo: Mark Griffin)

post. The climbing girl needs enough room in her skirt to climb, appropriate pants underneath it, and enough shoulder room in her dress to stretch. If she wears shoes they should be soft enough not to bruise her 'staircase' but have enough grip not to slip. The man's bent knee will be covered by the cloth of his trousers – but is that cloth strong enough to cope with being used as a stair carpet night after night? Will an object in the pocket of the trousers, or perhaps a button, buckle or belt, be pressed into his hipbone on the second 'step'? Will the pressure of the foot on the third 'elbow' stair cause the fabric to rip as it is used as a springboard for the final

jump, or will her foot slip on its silk or the silk slip on his body? If he's wearing a hat, what will happen when she puts her hand on his head, and will its brim get in the way when she sits on his shoulder?

Left to themselves, performers will sort out these problems and make the movements work, and they are good at surmounting physical difficulties. But they may sort them out at the expense of the design, since that is not their problem or in their eyeline: it is in the view of the director and designer, as the eyes of the audience. Careful fittings and enough of them, and forethought, prevent the design being spoilt by the necessities of

Testing the set, ease and stability of trousers, shirt and braces at a final fitting.

movement. There may not be time at the dress rehearsal to address these issues, remake costumes or redirect the movement.

Most companies use a stage manager, or someone other than actors or a designer to organize the timing of fittings. If, however, they are not used to working with physical theatre, particularly in the sort of company where time and rehearsal room space are in short supply, it may be difficult for them to realize how much contact the designer or maker needs with the performer, and how much the costume affects the movement and often the safety of performers. Formal fittings in a workroom away from the rehearsal room may take up a lot of the actors' time, and not be nearly as productive as stolen moments in rehearsal when the performer can wear a half-finished garment, try a particular move with the

maker watching, and hand it back with a quick comment.

FITTINGS DURING REHEARSAL

You have to be careful and subtle not to disturb the concentration of rehearsal, and check with both stage manager and director that they do not mind such a casual approach. There may be moments during warm-ups, or when there are rigging problems to be sorted out, when you can steal an actor for a quick fitting if you are on the spot. Complicated fittings or long, concentration-disturbing discussions about costume have no place in the rehearsal room. But once everyone sees and feels the benefit of the many small adjustments you can make without causing disruption, with a silent needle and thread and a pair of scissors, your presence will be

Make sure that stitching stretches as much as the fabric – be brutal with it. Better it should break in the rehearsal room than reveal all on stage.

welcomed and accepted. If it is not, you will have to go back to the pre-arranged, formally scheduled fittings, and just have more of them.

Unfortunately these often interrupt rehearsal time more, and take more time, than is usual or expected. Fittings may have to be in the rehearsal room, as seeing the performers in costume on the equipment is the only way to test the fit and practicality of the clothes. Some movements cannot be tried safely unless the actors have warmed up their bodies, and technicians are available to manage the equipment. Furthermore, if the movements of the action are complicated or risky, costumes may need many fittings and trials before they work. It is often quicker to bodge up a rough costume in cheap cloth as a trial until you see exactly what is required.

Specific Fittings

FITTINGS AND FASTENINGS ON TROUSERS

The shape of the bottom varies a great deal between individuals, even if they wear the same size trousers. Pay particular attention to the fit of the back seam, and shape it to fit closely to the shape of the buttocks and to the spine at the waist: this seam is the mainstay for keeping trousers in the correct place on the body.

Legs look longer and more elegant if the trouser hem is cut on a slant, so that it is longer at the back than at the front.

Make plackets for fastenings as short as is practicable. It is safer and more comfortable to have fewer fastenings that risk digging in, breaking or catching on rigging and equipment, even if it requires the most athletic wriggling to squeeze into the trousers.

It may be a budgetary necessity to use high street bought trousers, although these are often cut too low for movements requiring a supple waist. However, this can be resolved by removing the waistband and adding a band of matching cloth to increase its height.

Breeches must either be cut with a wide enough knee band to slip over the knee, or with enough bag to allow a full knee bend without straining the cloth over the knee. If breeches are cut in a stretch cloth they should have a close-fitting knee band with a slight stretch and elastic braces; this allows for the 10cm (4in) or so difference in the measurement between waist and hem when the knee is flexed and when the actor is standing straight.

Fastenings on trousers for some highly physical work may need to be moved to unusual places around the waist – for instance, a front fastening may not be comfortable for some work that calls for forward rolling over a bar. A fastening placed equidistantly between hipbone and front seam may be unusual, but it will lie on a soft part of the body and will not press on a bone.

Fastenings on the side seams (traditionally the left side) should be as flat as possible to avoid an uneven or wrinkled line.

Fastenings down the back seam can accentuate a beautiful spine and bottom, but must be very secure.

Use good quality thread, and double stitch all seams around the crotch, bottom and thighs. The most likely place for seams to split is where they cross each other, so reinforce these with double stitching and even tape.

There is no standard position for braces to be attached, though both sides must be equal in length and position. Set the front positions first and the back position afterwards. Braces should have some stretch: they can be all or partially elastic, and if they do not show, are better stitched firmly into the correct position after fitting, rather than buttoned. Do not trust clip-on braces, though they are very useful for fittings.

Braces should either cross at the back or have a strap across the back at mid-arm level, so they do not slip down over the shoulders during the action.

Braces on women's trousers, leggings or tights should not squash the bust and alter its natural shape. This may mean that they have to be set wider apart at waist level, with a cross strap at the back to prevent them from slipping. Crossing the elastic at the front between the breasts can work as long as this is not visible to the audience.

FITTING SKIRTS

Make sure the wearer is standing upright and looking straight ahead when you mark a hemline. Remember the eyeline level of the audience may not be the same as yours: people in the front row of the stalls look up at the performers and consequently up their skirts.

Test the width of the skirt by asking the performer to try out all the moves that might be prohibited if it were

The progress of a period swimsuit concealing a harness. 1) The first fitting of the harness. 2) Trial flight in harness with the costume pinned. 3) Fitting the costume in flight. 4) The choreographer works with the actor in costume. 5) Costume adjustments in rehearsal. 6) Working in costume in character.

Shoemakers and menders have sewing machines, which will cope with situations yours may not manage.

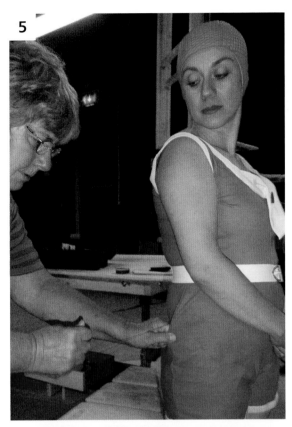

not wide enough; this will also give you the chance to see how the skirt moves.

FITTING AND FASTENING BODICES AND BLOUSES

For women performers, always fit bodices and blouses over the bra they will be wearing in performance. If the budget allows, find out the style and make of bra the performer prefers to work in, and buy it on the budget; then you can feel free to stitch, dye and cut it as you please.

The best way to make sure wide-necked costumes do not slip off the shoulders is to attach them to the bra or braces. Small tape loops that will fasten round the bra straps can be attached to the shoulder seam. They can be made, or bought in haberdashery stores. Sometimes a narrow tape from shoulder to shoulder at the back will stop a wide-necked top from slipping off the shoulders.

A tape is commercially available that will stick costumes to the skin; this is useful where a low-necked top gapes during a forward bending movement.

FITTING AND FASTENING UNDERPANTS

Underpants should only reveal as much as is acceptable for the role: if you can see them, then so can the audience, and they are consequently part of the costume. Therefore make sure that they are big enough to cover everything they need to for the performance, and that they stay in place and do not slip or wrinkle during movements. Check from the viewpoint of the audience in the front row that you cannot see up the legs.

If a young performer seems reserved about testing the decency of pants at a fitting, suggest they take them home and check for themselves in the mirror or in front of a trusted friend.

FITTING BODYSUITS

Extreme movements are sometimes needed in the action, such as crouching with the knees together with the head well down and the arms stretched out in front, sitting on the floor with the legs wide apart and holding each foot with both hands and the head on the knees, or doing a backbend. Check that if the performer is wearing a bodysuit they can do all these comfortably, then check that they can stand up without looking a wrinkled mess.

If the performer is not a standard size it can be more successful to fit separate tights or leggings, sleeveless or legless bodies, and close-fitting T-shirts.

Check that the suit does not pull at the crotch or shoulder when the actor curls up – if it does, the shoulder must be let out, or an extra piece added in the crotch.

FITTING DRESSES

If the waist of a dress is close-fitting or elastic, make sure that it does not ride up when the arms are raised and then get stuck: in some roles it can seem perfectly natural for the performer to pull down and tidy up her dress after a movement, but in others this may not seem appropriate.

There must be enough spread across the shoulders at the back to allow for the outstretched hands to be moved palm to palm, up and down in front of the body. There must also be enough room for the performer to circle her bent elbows at the same time in any direction.

FITTING JACKETS AND COATS

The length you choose to make a jacket can appear to alter the proportions of the actor who wears it. Look at him from a short distance away and see which length suits best, either for the look of the person or the role he is performing. It depends on the relative length of nape to waist, and waist to ground.

If the jacket or coat is worn buttoned there must be enough ease in the shoulders, arm and waist for the garment to move on the body; a close-fitting jacket can be used if it can be worn unbuttoned to accommodate some movements.

Checks at Fittings

The following checks should be made for the relevant articles of costume.

TROUSERS AND BREECHES

Can the actor squat and bend and kick his legs freely?

Is there enough spread in the crotch for sideways leg movements?

Do trousers slip down at the back after a squat, or do the legs stay caught up on calf muscles after a bend?

Are the fastenings in the right place, and the placket or fly as short as possible?

Do braces stay comfortably on the shoulders through violent movement?

Is the length neither too long nor too short?

Does the knee band on breeches fit correctly?

Can the actor bend his knee to his chest in breeches?

Do underpants stay in place, look decent from all angles through all movements, and not show a line under costumes?

Can the audience see up the legs of shorts in certain movements?

BODIES, DUNGAREES AND LEOTARDS

Can the actor curl up into a ball whilst squatting with the hands stretched in front of him, or crossed and curled round his body?

Do the shoulder seams or straps stay in place during violent movement?

SHIRTS, BLOUSES AND JACKETS

Can the actor stretch the arms up, forwards, out and down, and bend without things coming untucked?

Can the actor stretch his shoulders and arms backwards without making the front fastenings gape?

Can the actor roll his head round without the collar feeling restrictive?

Can the actor turn upside-down without his costume acting as a blindfold?

DRESSES

Can the actor turn upside-down without her costume covering her eyes?

Does the dress return to position after an upward stretch?

Check leg movements and pants.

Can the actor stretch the arms up, forwards, out and down?

Can the actor stretch the shoulders and arms backwards without making front fastenings gape?

Keep an elastic hair band on your wrist for keeping actors' hair out of the way when fitting collars, shoulders, etc.

Shoes

All performers need to feel right in their shoes. Quite apart from the way they look to the audience, shoes affect the gait, the posture, the height and the sound of the footsteps. They are an instant guide to period and character, and for many actors they offer a way of settling into the role they are playing. This is easy to understand. An actor looks in the mirror at a fitting and sees, not themselves, but the character they are playing. If you watch them you will see them instinctively adapt the way they place the weight and balance of their bodies to become the character. This process starts in the belly and breath and with the spine and shoulders. The feet take little part in this transformation. But as soon as they move their focus from the mirror and start walking, the feet in their shoes join in the process, and carry with them the memory of the character the actor saw in the mirror.

This aid to creating a character, so essential to naturalistic actors, is not always available to physical performers, as the different sorts of floor surface and the different sorts of movement need different shoes. Physical performers, as well as dancers, have to take care of their feet. The jolting pressure on the joints of the body produced by jumps and falls is considerable, and shoes must protect and be safe and appropriate to equipment during the course of a performance; a performer may need to wear robust jazz trainers for work on an unsprung floor, and then change into supple gymnastic pumps for a slack-wire walk. The shoes have to be chosen primarily for the process rather than the character, and they have to fit well and securely.

The initial fitting of bought shoes should happen on a clean surface. As soon as a physical performer puts on shoes or boots, their first action will not be to look at them, but to jump in them. If they do this on a dirty surface and then decide that the size is wrong, you will not be able to take them back to the shop and exchange them. Once you are sure you have the right size, the performer should run, jump and slide to make sure the shoes are right for their job. Although all shoes become

more supple and more comfortable with wear, if they feel wrong at the fitting they will probably go on causing problems. These may not become evident until the tech. and dress rehearsals, when performers wear their shoes for many hours. Even a slight discomfort will grow, possibly into a blister or painful place, and because of the subsequent performances this will not have time to heal.

The following advice may be helpful:

* Heel grips, little moons of grippy fabric stuck inside the upper back of the shoe, can sort out small problems such as a slipping heel.
* Leather or shoe expander dabbed on the inside and outside of the shoe where it is tight, will stretch that particular area.
* Replacing laces with elastic may help a quick shoe change.
* Non-slip soles can be glued to the sole of a slipping shoe.
* Shoes can be dyed with shoe dye, or painted or dipped in fabric dye if they are made of a suitable fabric.
* New shoes can be made to look old and decrepit with grease, oil, paint and different laces, but beware of weakening them.

Sort out shoes as early as you can so that comfort and safety can be tried and tested in rehearsal on the floor and equipment. Some dance work on an uncompromising floor can grind its way through shoes at an alarming rate, and you may find that after two or three days' rehearsal the shoes look as if they have been worn for months and are ready for the dustbin. In this case, unless you have a big enough budget to buy new ones every week, think again.

Many performers, movement directors and choreographers prefer bare feet, since toes need a finger-like grip on some equipment. There is often a necessary compromise between the sort of shoes, as a designer, you would like the actor to wear, and the sort of shoes the movement demands.

Changing the laces of shoes can change their appearance – big ribbon bows or strict round shoelaces can make the same shoes look very different.

The Performer's Jacket

A performer, who is also a juggler, a slack rope walker and an aerialist, needs a jacket. This must look casual and perfectly ordinary when we see him on stage, but it must also have concealed in it a dozen or so different pockets, some of which interconnect and will hold different-sized balls, handkerchiefs and batons. It also has to hide a harness with which he will be hooked on to a point, which will whirl him round the stage in the air.

There is no way that this can be cut and made right first time. For a start, the performer cannot know what is possible until he can use the pockets. The designer/maker can invent with him possibilities of concealment and revelation by rough stitching or safety pinning in pockets their concealed tubes and extensions that will be tried out in rehearsal.

The harness, which will be built into the lining of the jacket, will stiffen and interfere with the smooth inside of the jacket, and there will have to be a hole at the back of the neck for a rigging point. In the light of this it is decided that there will have to be two jackets that look exactly alike to the audience, but contain different tricks – one for the aerial work and one for the juggling.

The mock-up juggling jacket is made and fitted as carefully as any normal jacket, but it has as many pockets as can be fitted into it, many more than the wearer could use. These may not be the right size or in the right place, but will give the performer choice and the maker something tangible to work on, and may produce extra ideas in rehearsal and play that neither had thought of in advance.

A pattern is kept – an exact copy of the fitted jacket made in calico or white cotton, on which all the rough changes to pockets and fit are marked: it will be the template for the real jacket and the pattern for the second one that conceals the harness.

Once the movements have been set, a strong version is made from the pattern with all the alterations in

place, in a fabric of the same weight as the finished one, but without its expensive cloth or careful and lengthy detail and finishing. This is a rehearsal jacket, and in this the final small adjustments will be made.

This jacket is a collaborative piece of invention between performer, designer and maker, and without it the performance with all its tricks will not be possible. To the audience it is a garment they will hardly notice; to the juggler it is as essential as his juggling balls, and to the designer and maker the most satisfying and demanding work of collaboration.

The jacket in performance: (left) juggling, (right) flying. (Photos: Patrick Baldwin)

9 Costume for Extreme Physical Movement

Practical Research for Physical Work

The costume designer for any sort of extreme physical work adds another layer of research to the gathering of information about the era, place, content and style that is involved in any costume design preparation process. The performers' safety, as well as their comfort and bodily freedom, become involved. Inventive solutions to cutting and fitting problems that occur when performers move in costume are increased when the movement becomes extreme. For instance, the designer of a blouse for an actress in a naturalistic play does not have to imagine that they might cause serious injury to its wearer. A blouse cut to a usual pattern, when worn by a girl whirling her body down a rope like a controlled propeller, can begin to wind into the rope and become so entangled during the descent that she is left dangling like a fly on a cobweb metres above the ground.

A picture of the girl with delicious ruffles down the front of her bodice might fly into your head, but it must fly out just as quickly and be replaced by a taut garment with a strong, flat front which lies close to the body. Though the ruffles may have been rejected as impractical, the instinct that inspired them can remain and be translated into a more practical form: thus the colour and pattern of the cloth could reflect the light-heartedness of a frill; ruffled cap sleeves, safely away from the winding danger of the rope, could be designed with a

St Mary's University College in *Klockwerk*. (Photo: Lisette Barlow)

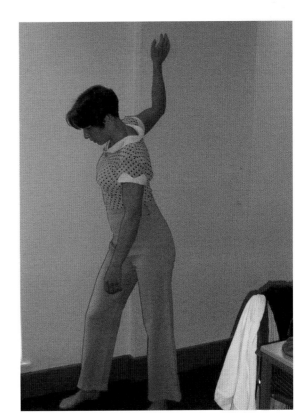

Blouse and trousers cut to withstand extreme movement and harsh equipment.

flirtatious flip; a wavy-edged peplum that begins its curving line away from the front of the body could give grace and ornamentation to the cut of the blouse.

Imagination, and a visual recall of the way limbs and muscles move in different circumstances, can hint at the

Meline
Every Action.
09.

trouser
high with
braces.

The sweater is a close fitting and much more sophisticated version of the tank-top. It's backed on power-net for stability.

blouse opening with tank top all back

slits reveal bright green facings

TB.

Costume designed for the life it will lead.

lurking risks of certain manoeuvres – but the only people who really know what happens to their bodies whilst working on a particular piece of circus equipment or when lifting their partner in a dance movement, are the performers themselves. They are the experts with whom your research into the safety of your design must begin and end, since their health and working life depends on their expertise. Though experience can warn them that certain features of a costume might cause trouble in action, they cannot tell exactly what will hinder and what

Very few people are allergic to silk or cotton, but many are allergic to wool.

will help without trying the moves on the equipment. They must have time to do so, and you must expect that changes and adaptations will be inevitable as the costumes begin their hard and demanding working life.

ROUNDSLINGS, ROPES, HOOKS, FASTENINGS

Many of these come with safety and weight checks in place. If you sew through the actual fabric of some of these you will affect its internal integrity and consequently its safety; others can be stitched without damage. Hooks and karabiners and suchlike, which may have to be built into the costume, have a prescribed safe working load.

There are times when formally rated circus equipment is not used, in which case always overestimate the amount of stress that may be put on stitching, fabric and fastenings, remembering that the apparent weight of an object when still is much less than when it is moving or bouncing. Also remember that each stitch is a perforation of the fabric and will weaken it, so it may be necessary to make a prototype that can be weight-tested before its first trial. And, of course, test and test again, with the performers near the ground and with crash mats.

Designing to Accommodate Harness

There are many different types of harness used for different purposes, and you will need specialized information to get the right one for the job. You will get the clearest response if you know what effect the director wants to achieve. An actor being hung on the gibbet will need a different harness from one who is somersaulting through the air as Puck. You will need to know if they are to fly on a track or on a pulley, and what they will be rigged to. You have to approach this purchase from a safety and practicality angle first, and work in the aesthetics afterwards. Make sure you know all the possibilities, and have checked with both the movement director, someone who really knows about harness work, and the safety technician before you make your choice.

Harnesses attach performers to structures and equipment to stop them falling. They may be just for safety purposes, but they are used in performance to make people appear to float, fly and defy gravity. They challenge the designer as they are often bulky and awkward to conceal under or within a costume, and the rigging points, wherever they are, are lumpy and ugly. You must see the performer in the harness attached to the equipment in the way they will be in the show in order to understand how it will affect the design, where the costume will have to conceal rigging, and where you can give your design ideas free rein.

Imagine a performer in harness clipped to a rope from a rigging point between his shoulders at the back of the neck. As his weight is lifted from the ground the balance of his body alters. Ask him to simply hang there with no action: you will see that his body tips forward, his legs go up behind and the harness tightens with the weight. The angle of attachment at the rigging point alters. Any controlled movement the performer makes again alters the angles of the rigging clips.

Imagine then cutting a jacket with a hole at the back of the neck to allow for the attachment and its movement. If it is not big enough to allow for the change in angle, the jacket will rise to a point at the back of the neck and the line of the spine will be lost to the audience. Then imagine you have cut the hole big enough. When the performer is de-rigged and standing naturally, still in the harness but without the pull of the rigging, the jacket will have a hole in the back. It is a lot easier to decide what to do about this hole at the design stage so that the costume can be cut to allow for the problem, than to address it later when a bodged solution may ruin the purity of your design.

Costume for any of the type of work loosely classified as 'circus' can be a disguise for quite specialist equipment. A performer may look as if she is in ordinary clothes, but her dress may be concealing harness, or clips, or some safety device that is necessary for the sort of work she will do. Think of the famous flying scene in *Peter Pan*: the children are in their nursery wearing pyjamas and nightdress, and at the end of the scene they fly out of the window. It is every child's dream to fly, and it is every designer's dream that the lumpy safety

---

If your machine doesn't have a setting for stretch sewing, use a small zigzag stitch.

equipment strapped and buckled on these children should not be seen by the audience. However, the equipment and rigging that enables the magic to happen is rigorously controlled and not to be tampered with, since safety and insurance can both be compromised if any alteration is made to the structure of the harness.

Before you so much as put a needle through a bit of webbing you must check that the safety rating will not be affected. In most cases you can cover the harness and disguise it in a variety of ways, and adjust any padding. You may be allowed to shorten some straps once the harness has been fitted if they are dangling about on a small performer, but always be cautious and ask before you do. But there are ways of designing costumes to conceal the lumps and bumps of buckles and rigging points, and of using colour changes and different textures to attract the audience's eyes away from any necessary rigging bulges.

It is essential to check out different sorts of harness with both the movement director who is designing the movement that will take place in the harness, and the person who has the technical knowledge to advise on and ensure both the safety of the performer and the practicality of performing the moves when wearing it. Of course a designer wants the lightest construction with the least lumpy rigging points, but there are other factors to consider. A harness may look light and uncluttered when the actor is standing on the ground, but it may tend to move on the body as the rig, rather than the performer's feet, supports their bodyweight. The more the harness can hold the body firmly around the torso, the less likely it is to shift about when the actor is flying, and the better you will be able to hide it under the costume.

Actors who are not used to wearing a harness – although they may be used to, and uncomplaining about, the awkwardness of performing in tight period corsets or hot, padded doublets – are often surprised by the discomfort of harness work, and it can be difficult to convince them that although you might be able to make things less painful, you cannot magic away the discomfort.

The rigging points need to be looked at carefully with regard to the design of the covering costume. The neater and less obtrusive they are on the smooth silhouette of the body, the better for the costume. This may be a question of choosing, for instance, a harness with a built-in swivel point at the hips rather than a loop to which a swivel and a karabiner will have to be attached.

The fastenings offer further chances for choice. They all have to be safe, but may be laces, buckles or clips, all of which have a different appearance and different behaviour. A lot will depend on how long the actor has to get into and out of the harness, who is there to help them, and how much opportunity they have both had to rehearse the process.

It is best to have the harness first and to design the costume when you know what it has to conceal, and how it must be cut to avoid becoming entangled in rigging, or equipment. It is also necessary to do at least one fitting when the performer is actually hanging in the harness, although just off the floor where you can reach them: that is the only way you can tell how harness and fabric and actor's body will all move together, and adjust the fit accordingly. You will also need a further fitting when the actor is flying and you can see how costume and movement work together.

Costume for Lifts, Throws and Drops

Most physical performance has some moment when one person will carry or climb on another. There are hundreds of different sorts of lift involving different numbers of people with different balance, throws or drops. The ones that most concern a costume designer are those where the clothes might impede the action or obscure the vision of the performer.

Costume worn when balancing on someone's head or shoulders may need to be designed so that it does not obscure the vision of the supporting performer. Fullness can become twisted and entangled during the lifting process, but if the lifted person ends up with one leg each side of the carrier's head, the skirt must be cut with enough fabric to allow it to pass behind the neck of the

Your own spit on your own blood will get the stain off – nobody else's will do it as well.

Costume designed as casual street wear but with hidden technical adaptations for cling and grip. (Photo: Nik Mackey)

carrier, otherwise it will obscure his vision by falling over his eyes.

Performers will tread on each other using the thigh of a bent leg, a hipbone, or any angle created by the body as a step or foothold, and hard shoes cause pain and bruises. Unsecured fabric will naturally fall downwards, and as physical performers spend a lot of their time upside-down, this has to be considered or a skirt can become a blindfold.

Costume acts as a layer of protection for the body, and can disguise the pads and strapping that are used to protect from and support injury. Knee padding can be essential for some performers, and trousers must be designed so that an ugly lump does not ridge the fabric covering them. Different layers of fabric may slip on each other or on the skin, making the sort of precise lift used in acrobalance difficult to perform.

The costume design should be structured so that the actual points where hands grasp or catch the body are free from anything that might preclude smooth and secure action. The performers will know what the actions feel like, and you, watching, will know what they look like, so the costume design will be influenced by the balance of these observations.

Problems with Flaps and Fullness

Loose fabric around the torso causes problems on some equipment, particularly on poles, ropes or silks: the fabric can twist and bind, and in extreme cases spiral itself round a rope or pole so tightly that the only way out may be to cut or rip the cloth. Loose fabric anywhere on the body can cause trouble, and the likely places for it to do so will be different on different equipment. The skirt over the bloomers that hide a harness could get between the hands and bar of a trapeze artist. The performers will know, and their choice of training clothes will give designers clues, and lead to a design that is practical as well as beautiful and apt.

The way extra fabric moves against other fabrics can also be problematic, because it can slip or grip as it can on skin; so although the extra protection of a double layer of fabric can be useful as padding, it must be tried out in a rehearsal situation to make sure that it is not more trouble than it is worth. It might just roll itself into a bruising lump between the body and the equipment, or the layers might shift against each other, making grip difficult.

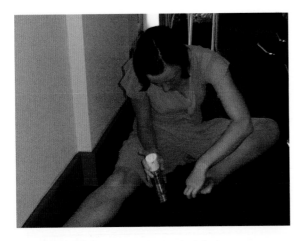

The aerialist sticks her tights to her feet to prevent slipping.

Regulating Temperature

Circus rehearsal spaces are often big and high and consequently expensive to heat; nevertheless that is where most of the later fittings will take place. The performers are constantly putting on and taking off layers of rehearsal clothes to keep muscles at a good working temperature – but they cannot do this in performance when the lights and the audience mean the temperature at which they are working is very different, and usually much hotter. The combination of the rising hot air and being close to the light source means that it is a hot job.

Sweat and hard wear mean that it is often necessary to make doubles of costumes, as they can get wringing wet in performance. Many of the stretch fabrics do not absorb sweat well, or allow the skin to breathe through the cloth. You can tell how a fabric will react to sweat by dropping a teaspoon of water on the inside of the cloth and seeing how quickly it sinks in, or if it tends to sit on the surface. Some fabrics will absorb water from one side and not from the other.

Actors are used to being too hot in costume, particularly period costume, but for circus performers overheating can be risky as well as uncomfortable. Heat means sweat, and sweat can mean dehydration and consequent loss of energy if the work is very vigorous, and can make both skin and the equipment slippery. The balance needs to be struck between protecting the body and overheating it. Furthermore everyone sweats differently: some people get slippery hands and feet, while others drip sweat into eyes or soak clothes, which makes the cloth cling to their skin rather than slip over it.

Once again, although performers can predict the sort of sweat problems they are likely to have, they do not know for certain until they have tried. A performer whose hands sweat a lot, and whose work needs a secure grip, will enjoy a costume made of absorbent fabric so that they can wipe wet hands on it just before a move without the audience seeing. Grip problems can be pre-empted by spraying hands or feet with the grip-improving spray used by gymnasts, or by rubbing dry resin (hardened tree sap sold in music shops for violin bows) into the hands. An extra grippy mixture can be made by mixing a solution of dry resin and surgical spirit almost to a point of saturation.

Coping with Skin Injuries

Many moves on circus equipment, particularly on ropes, can cause friction burns or can scrape, blister or callus the skin. Any part of the body which can be used as a hook is prone to hurt – the hocks or elbows, ankles, waist and the armpits, particularly when the rope or silk is hooked round the back of the neck and under the arms. Moreover repeated rehearsal and performance of a move can damage a section of skin which never has the chance to get better.

This friction of skin on cloth or equipment may need protecting: rope is a fierce burner of sliding skin, but quite often a very thin, close-fitting layer of fabric will protect these areas, as thin as a pair of sheer tights that cannot be seen by the audience. A thin body or leotard and leggings are often worn under costume so that there will always be two layers of fabric protecting the skin. Circus performers and dancers make very little fuss about physical discomfort, and accept it as part of the job, and quite often do not mention something that is very

Hair spray on the buttocks will keep pants in place.

Cocktail dress designed
for aerial movement.
(Photos: Nik Mackey)

uncomfortable or even painful. The more a designer or maker can find out about these possible pains, the more they will be able to design the costume to prevent them occurring.

Costumes can be cut in a way that looks natural but works as protection. Thus inner sleeves or a firm, flat doubling-up or interlining of cloth over a joint that is at

risk of injury can stop a painful place developing. Performers will have invented all sorts of tricks of their own to protect themselves in rehearsal, and these can be adapted and incorporated into the costume as long as you know about them in advance. You may not be told about them, and may have to ask. It is not only the actors' comfort that makes this information useful: the stress points that cause pain are usually the places where a costume is liable to wear and tear, so it can be strengthened in advance to cope with its tough life.

Positioning Pockets

Pockets, if they are necessary, need to be carefully positioned. They can work like a hook and get caught on anything that sticks out from the set or the equipment, in the same way that you might catch a pocket on a door handle. They can trap and sprain fingers, thumbs and toes. However, they are also an adaptable, portable, convenient hidden space that a performer can keep with

him. They can be expanded inside a garment to hide props, be lined with waterproof cloth for a particular effect, or work as a trickle effect for water or sand.

Pockets can be joined inside like a tube from outlet to outlet so that something dropped into one pocket can appear from another. If an actor with pockets in his costume has to turn upside-down the pocket may have to have an internal pillowcase-like flap to prevent its contents tumbling to the floor.

Pockets do not have to be placed in conventional places. The angle at which a pocket is set can be important. You can tell the most convenient place to position pockets by asking an actor to imagine putting a small

A collection of flat- and round-edge buttons.

Store up strong, flat buttons in all sizes – it can take a long time to source correct ones when you need them.

The impact of a hairstyle is immediate for the audience. (Photo: Alex Byrne)

object in his pocket and marking the instinctive position and angle of his hands. It may be that the best place to conceal a stick-like prop is in a long thin pocket which runs from the nape of the neck to the small of the back; the gesture that then will produce the prop may be obvious but can be elegant. A pocket on the inside of a jacket almost under the arm will conceal the bulk of a surprise prop, and sometimes the trouser leg rather than the conventional hip may be a more useful place. An extra lining to the bottom of the sleeve finishing with a hidden elastic wristband makes a good cache for small items. Tailcoats traditionally have two capacious pockets in the tails. When small props have to be produced quickly or in succession it can help the actor to have a division in the pocket to keep things separate.

It can help an actor find the entrance to a pocket in a full garment if you back one side of the opening with a tape or fabric stiffer than the fabric of the garment: then he will find it and achieve what he needs to do with a natural movement rather than a searching fumble.

Selecting Trimmings

Thought must go into trimmings, into buckles, buttons and braid. They are an aesthetic punctuation to the design of a costume, but are often lumpy and hard. Buckle against bone can be as bruising as rolling over a stone; buttons and hooks can latch or catch in awkward places, and rolling on a cord trim can feel like rolling on a stick.

Buttons can cause bruises and should be as flat as possible. The best, if you can get hold of them, are old-fashioned 'laundry buttons' which are strong, flat and covered in linen and which you can dye to any colour. Buttons or buckles catching can tear silks and other expensive cloth equipment. It is sometimes better, if you want the look of a buckle without its bruising and catching potential, to make a mock one from braid or paint and conceal a flat and practical fastening underneath it.

'Memento Mori'

Two performers, a man and a woman, perform the dance of death on a rectangular suspended frame. The atmosphere of the work is calm, slow and dark, and the movement, music and lighting have an eerie gravitas. The understated power and the dark attraction to the beauty and inevitability of death are held in every moment of the piece. Although the inspiration for the work comes from Holbein's sixteenth-century woodcuts, where death is represented as a skeleton dancing his contemporary characters to their graves, the company have created a work that is as timeless as its subject.

Despite this contemporary treatment, a feeling of the rich dark colour and texture of Tudor life remains stubbornly at the heart of the design concept. The woman must have a formality of style, and will wear a red velvet dress, long sleeved and formal, in contrast with the apparent nakedness of Death. However real the dress looks, it has to work in performance. The design is close and clinging, and shows every line of the body as the velvet catches the light. Consequently the fabric, whilst looking rich and luxurious, must stretch and be very tough. The length has to be precise – just on the knee to free the hocks, which means that pants must be made out of the same fabric. The skirt of the dress has to be attached to the pants at the side seams so that it does not flap over the face on any upside-down moves, or reveal itself as a separate garment more than can be helped. The sleeves, designed long for formality, have to be shortened to below the elbow to allow the man's hands to grip her wrists securely enough to be safe. A thin, invisible sleeve made of a cut pair of tights is added to protect her arms. Her legs are protected by flesh-coloured tights with the feet cut off. A designer can work on an idea from a distance. But none of these adaptations to the original design could have been made without seeing the performers trying the moves on the equipment in costume.

Colour and light underline the aerial drama. (Photo: Nik Mackey)

The Impact of Hairstyle

The designer thinks about the hair with the costume. It is very difficult for a performer, or indeed anyone, to recognize from a mirror the way they will look on stage, and this is particularly true with reference to hair. People's hair, beards and moustaches are their own property, and although you can suggest styles that you think would work well for a particular role, you have to remember that the performer does have to live with their hair off stage, and when it is a question of a particular cut it has to be a mutual decision. Beards and moustaches are similarly part of the costume design and can be shaved and cut to change the shape and proportions of a face.

Eyebrows can change the look of the face, and the shadow of the brow often creates the strongest line of the face in stage light. Performers cannot see this for themselves, and have to rely on outside eyes and not their mirrors to know the most expressive and visible eyebrow line on stage.

The shape of the head, and the way the head tilts and turns on the neck, has a strong effect on the beauty and expressive power of movement. The size of the head, and its relative balance to the proportions of the rest of the body, is changed by the hairstyle. The curve of the neck into the shoulder on a female body, the column of a man's neck and throat, the way the curve of the spine supports the head, and the shadow of the line of the jaw, are all given a lovely definition by the physical training of the bodies of these performers, and it is a waste to hide this from the audience behind a concealing hairstyle. It can also be a waste to screw the hair up in a tight, hard ballet bun, which may reveal the lines but throws away all the lively extension of movement which hair can show.

Most physical performers tie up long hair when rehearsing, and it is easy to forget that hair is as affected by gravity and swing in the same way as fabric, and can be just as beautiful and dangerous. The sight of an upside-down girl swinging through the air, the line of her body extended by the sweep of her long hair, must be rehearsed as well as imagined if the audience is to see it. Long hair can look great on a forward swing when the movement of the air takes it back from the face, but on a backward one it will become a hood.

Test wigs in every possible situation that might occur in the show to be certain that they will stay on and not slip. You cannot tell from a fitting, because during a lit performance the actor's head, so near light sources in aerial performance, may sweat and become more slippery. Wigs are hot to work in, and if they are supposed to look real, are expensive and need constant maintenance to continue to look good. It's best to avoid them if you can unless you are working with a generous budget, or know there will be someone travelling with the company who can keep them looking as good on the last performance as they did at the dress rehearsal.

These factors, and many more, must be allowed for at an early stage of the design. It is essential for costume designers for physical work to spend time in rehearsal and with the performers. Rehearsal time is used to develop the action, and there will be many movements that no one can possibly foresee. Even when the costumes have been designed and made with foresight and discussion there will be changes and adaptation. The more your designs have a built-in ability to absorb the changes, the more you are likely to get the pictures you imagine to appear in the final show.

Even if no other make-up is used, pale eyebrows need darkening to help the audience understand the actors' expression, particularly in side light.

10 Accessories, Extras and Costume Objects

Set and Costume Combinations

There are many occasions in physical theatre when the boundaries between set and costume are blurred. This may be because there is simply not enough room for anything other than the performers on stage, or that the movement of fabric is so visually interesting that it overwhelms other messages. The fluidity of fabric, as opposed to a more concretely constructed set, is often more appropriate and adaptable for a work that involves a lot of movement. It may not be appropriate to have a set change to a hayfield, but more useful to have a field suggested by costumed actors moving and dressed as a version of corn or grass in the wind than a constructed set. The nature of much devised physical work abstracts it from reality and naturalism, and lends itself to a more imaginative way of seeing and representing the world.

BELTS

Belts can have a specific use as a disguise for a strong rigging point. A harness that has straps round the thighs can be disguised by a belt that appears to be part of a normal dress. The webbing can all be under knickers under the skirt and emerge through slits at the waist where its buckles and rigging points can be disguised by the belt.

Buckles on belts can cause bruises if they are rolled on, and they can also catch on equipment. It is sometimes better to disguise a flatter fastening with a pretend, flat buckle made out of fabric.

The waist is the thinnest part of the torso and also relatively soft. This makes it a good place to emphasize with a belt, particularly if the rest of the costume is loose.

Take care not to make wide belts too stiff, as they may be uncomfortable on forward or sideways movements. Also check that wide elastic does not roll up when stretched: some will end up as an uncomfortable cord round the waist. Some elastic is made so that it does not roll: it is often called waistband elastic, and recognizable by the fact that it does not have lengthways stripes in the weave but a more complicated mossy or even look. Check before you buy by stretching half a metre and seeing if it rolls.

HATS

Most performers love wearing hats. Designers also love them, as their silhouette and decoration are an excellent way of setting class, status, era and so on. Problems with hats include how to make them stay on, how to stop them stealing the light by shadowing a performer's eyes, and what to do with them on stage when you take them off. They have to be used in rehearsal or all three problems will take up valuable time at the technical rehearsal.

Cutting, stitching or folding, can alter the brims of felt hats.

Steaming over a kettle can alter the size. Pin a band of tape or ribbon round the crown to match the head measurement, plus a centimetre or two of ease. Then rest the hat on a steaming kettle or saucepan, and stretch or pinch-shrink the felt with your fingers to match the band.

St Mary's University College in *Visions and Delusions*. (Photo: Christine Jarvis)

Above: The hat conveys an era. (Photo: Christine Jarvis) Below: The same hat base adapted for different characters.

You can help a hat stay securely on the head by using an elastic under the chin, or more subtly, one that goes behind the head under the hair, or by pinning a flat curl in the hair and hat-pinning the hat to it.

It may help to stretch a 10–15cm (4–6in) piece of wide elastic inside the crown at the back, and stitch it in three places to the hat.

A slit can be cut over the fold of crown and brim, and a backing inserted to let out a hat that is too tight.

To make a hat smaller, folded paper or wadding can be put inside the inner band, or a strip of thin foam glued inside it.

Earrings and jewellery can sound loud when head mikes are used.

foam glued inside the hat to help it fit closely

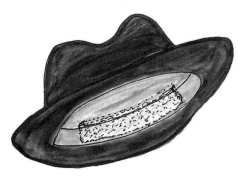

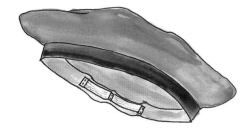

elastic stretched and stitched inside hat band to keep it on

Adjustments to hats.

SOCKS, STOCKINGS AND TIGHTS

Socks are a way of adding an occasional and subtle flash of colour as the knee bends and the trouser leg rolls up. Very short 'trainer socks' are a way of keeping the inside of the shoe clean, but make sure the rim does not show above the shoe unless you mean it to do so. It may seem unbelievable that in a huge theatre a centimetre of unwanted sock will be noticed, but it is true.

Choose socks with as high a percentage of cotton as possible, and buy two pairs for each character.

If you want the colour and look of thick woollen socks without the bulk over the foot, zigzag machine stitch a thin sock to it below the shoe line, cut the thick foot part away and add another round of zigzag stitching to secure and finish it off. Cutting the fabric after stitching will minimize the frilly stretch that can occur when sewing knitted cloth near its edge.

It may be necessary to cut away the toe and heel of socks or tights when the performer is working barefoot. On some surfaces they make feet slip or fail to grip. With

A bag of surprises.

some equipment the performer needs to use their toes, the big toes for leverage or the gap between the big toe and second toe as a slot for rope.

Light elastic braces can be added to tights if they slip down or wrinkle during performance.

An elastic strap under the instep can be added to cut-off tights if you have to cut the feet off them or if footless tights ride up after knee-bending moves.

BAGS

Bags are another of those items that are sometimes prop and sometimes costume. When they are carried by the performer on stage they are usually designed with the costume, and often in physical work have a function beyond their appearance. They are invaluable to designers and directors as an on-stage repository for tricks and concealment – rather like being able to carry around a trap door or a cupboard in a believable manner. They have another use as a sort of Christmas stocking for the designer to surprise performers during an improvisation – who doesn't want to open a bag and see what is inside?

The way they are carried, and the way they open and shut on stage, and what is in them, must be thought about and rehearsed.

An empty bag almost always looks empty, even when the audience cannot see inside it, and the weight must be real or mimed to look real.

A hoard of spectacles and a shoal of gloves.

SPECTACLES

The earpieces of spectacles can be extended with millinery wire or other soft and covered wire to keep them on during movement. Stretch straps for spectacles, designed to keep them in place for sporting activity, are available from sports suppliers.

An optician can replace lenses in glasses with clear glass if you need a realistic reflection of light from them.

Remove glass from spectacles by wrapping them in a cloth and hitting the centre of the glass with a small hammer. The glass stays in the cloth. Check that the inside rim is smooth and glass free before use.

HOODS

Check that hoods do not fall over the face or get in the way of upside-down movement, or hide the wearer's

face from the audience. Attach them between the shoulders with a stitch through the centre back seam if they are not worn over the head.

Make sure they are not so deep as to limit sideways vision, in the same way as blinkers on a horse. The hood can be fastened to the hair on the crown of the head with a small comb sewn to the fabric, or attached to an Alice band if it is up all the time.

A separate hood with a cowl (the rounded piece that falls over the shoulders) will need to be attached to the costume underneath at the shoulders and centre back to keep it in place.

GAITERS

Gaiters will protect the ankles from friction burns from ropes or bruising on equipment. Fit them carefully so that they sit close to the leg, and make sure the fastenings are secure and as flat as possible; velcro or lacing may be the best option. They usually have an instep strap to stop them slipping up or round the leg in action.

SHOES

A decision based on necessity and on the preference of the movement director and the performers, rather than the designer, may be made for the performers to work

Wings

A small pair of fairy wings hovering over the shoulder blades is straightforward, while larger lightweight fabric wings need to be fixed, perhaps at the nape, elbows and wrists, to catch the air as the actor moves. It is a different matter, however, when the wings are big and spread upwards and outwards, and must be supported by structure rather than air: these need careful attachment to the body. The first thing to decide, once you know what you want them to look like and their intended action, is how they will be attached. They are most likely to be successful if you create that structure first.

Wings that are made of anything but the lightest cloth and struts may need a corset-like bodice to which they can be attached. This should fit snugly and firmly and fasten securely so that you have a steadfast base for attachment. The height, length and breadth of the wingspan determines whether this is a short bodice that will only need the depth from nape to just under arm level, or whether it is a nape to below waist garment which can hold the struts of the structure against the back further down the spine.

Indoors, fast movement imbues wings with an inconvenient life of their own, and given half a chance they will behave like a wobbling kite. Out of doors it is even worse, so the air must be able to pass through the structure. Be realistic about the allowance you have to make for this – even netting will catch the wind.

Very large wings may have to be thought of more as puppets than costumes, and the performer may need sticks or struts from a waist belt to control them.

Wings in the making: a) the corsets; b) the struts; c) in performance. (Photo: Lisette Barlow)

in bare feet. Bare feet are often the only way they can work on particular types of equipment. For some styles of dance and movement the performers need the contact of their bare feet on the floor and the uninterrupted, expressive line of leg, ankle, heel and toes. This is great for the budget, which shoes often strain to disaster point, but may not be so good for the design.

If an actor in a suit has bare feet it says one of three things to an audience: he is not completely dressed and will put the shoes on later, he is eccentric in some way yet to be disclosed, or there is a suggestion of abstraction from reality in the style of the work. The third is the most likely way for a designer to get round the oddity of a barefoot person in a situation where, in a parallel and non-theatrical reality, he would wear shoes.

Different sorts of floor surface and different sorts of movement need different shoes, and there is often a necessary compromise between the sort of shoes which, as a designer, you would like the actor to wear, and the sort of shoes the movement demands. Physical performers, as well as dancers, have to take care of their feet, and the jolting pressure on the joints of the body produced by jumps and falls is considerably greater than that experienced in the normal running of life.

The designer must therefore be sympathetic if dancers seem over fussy about footwear, and not to care about the design aspect of this part of their costume. Their feet are as necessary to them in their job as your eyes. They have to look after them, and be conscious of the knock-on effects on the rest of their body of wearing the wrong shoes for the job. Many dancers have chronic knee, foot or other joint injuries but have found ways to protect them, and they know what will work for them. Nevertheless you can present alternatives for experiment that they may not have thought of or experienced before. Although you cannot force the issue, you can work round it with all the ingenuity you can muster to make sure the audience are not distracted from the message of the costume by the feet at the bottom of it.

The floor surface must also be considered. A dance floor is designed to be kind to performers' feet, but a lot of work happens in buildings where floors are hard, uneven or splintery, and shoes must be worn for health and safety reasons. Again the choice of shoe may have to depend more on the safety aspect than the design, and the designer will have to console himself with the knowledge that the audience would notice a lot more than feet if the performer fell and had to be carried off stage.

There is a huge choice of shoes designed for every aspect of dance and physical movement, many of which, such as the ballroom dance shoe and the jazz shoe, can pass or be disguised as everyday footwear. Others, such as the traditional blocked ballet shoe, will look like specialist dancewear whatever you do. Split sole dance trainers and some dance boots can cross the line between dancewear and street wear, and in certain cases become incorporated into the costume design. Shoes reappear through different eras and fashions, and the Oxford dance shoe on stage looks alike enough to any contemporary formal shoe to pass unnoticed. Similarly the canvas lightweight ballet pump or gym shoe can be disguised or dyed to look like a lightweight court shoe from a different era, and the character shoe is more or less 1920s without any further help.

Sport equipment shops sell styles that are suitable for movement and have the unusual or interesting shape which can work as part of a costume design. A huge range of shoes – such as surfing shoes, tabi (split-toe) shoes, rock climbing, boxing and riding boots – are designed for use in various sports or martial arts and can be adapted for theatre use. It is difficult to get the fitting of shoes right first time and if you cannot go with the performer to choose and try shoes, take a choice for the fitting and return the ones that you are not using.

Any work outdoors, or in a situation where the public uses the space as well as the performers, puts bare feet at risk. When working on a tight budget where there is a big cast to costume the only possibility may be the gym pumps or plimsolls that are sold in black or white for school wear, and made in all sizes for men, women and children, though the larger men's sizes may have to be

If there is not a person responsible for the wardrobe care during the run, find out which performer sews or mends best and beg them to take on the responsibility.

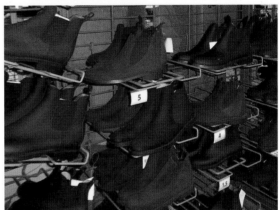

Sports shoes can be useful for stage work.

ordered. Their advantage, apart from the price, is that they are non-slip, and the white ones can be dyed in the washing machine to any colour.

A long run of performances will mean the added cost of replacing shoes, and this must be budgeted for. Concrete and other hard surfaces grind away at the soles, and shoes which may last a season on the street, will be shredded by a fortnight of dancing. For this reason, although performers may offer to wear their own shoes, and often prefer them, you need to budget for replacing them if they wear out during the run.

Make the show shoes available for performers to wear in rehearsal as soon as you can. There are bound to be problems of slip, grip and fit that will be hard to resolve in the last few days before the opening night. Shoes might feel fine at the fitting, but neither you nor the performer can tell until they are moving in rehearsal whether they will really be fit for the job, and it is worth taking a great deal of trouble to get this right. For many performers their shoes, and how they affect the movement and balance of their bodies, constitute a most important aspect of the character development of their role. No actors or performers, in any field or genre, do their best work when their feet feel wrong, and it is unfortunate for designers that this aspect of costume is often so expensive to get right, and so necessary.

Guard your fabric cutting scissors and have less valuable ones for people to borrow.

11 The Technical and Dress Rehearsal and the Show

At some point near the date of the first performance the content of the show will be more or less fixed in place. It is always 'more or less' with devised shows, as the habit of invention fights for its life till the bitter end and dies hard. There will be changes right up to the very last day, sometimes to the last hour in the actors' work on stage, though it is not often practical to adapt costume, set and objects so near the first night. The visual aspect of much of this genre of work means that technical rehearsals can be arduous for both cast and crew.

The lighting makes the world the performers have created in the rehearsal room a very different place. Powerful lights are on all day, heating up the space into a hot box which is sometimes pitch dark and sometimes blindingly bright. They may be able to see little beyond each other, and nothing at all of the audience or the wings. The lights which display them with such brilliant intensity to the audience can dazzle them, and make it difficult to see entrances and exits in the space, and hand- and footholds on some equipment.

Attention is focused on the technicalities of the show and not on the quality of the performers' work. They have to hang around on stage in costume and make-up keeping their muscles warmed up to do any move they are asked to. They will be told to move a pace to the right or to the left for a reason the lighting designer can see

RedCape Theatre in *From Newbury With Love*. (Photo: Nik Mackey)

but they cannot, and wait while volume levels that sound different on stage are set for the ears of the audience. A technician walks on, does something purposeful with a spanner or stares up at the grid, shouts a number and walks off. Silence, and then a slight change in the light or the murmur of a technical discussion in the auditorium too far away for them to hear. There will be long periods when nothing at all appears to be happening, and times when they must change in and out of costume over and over again to perfect the timing of a quick change.

Meanwhile the auditorium and the backstage area is a hive of concentrated activity as every technical aspect is addressed, resolved and noted. Full costume, if it has not been used in rehearsal, may be more restrictive and hotter or colder than training clothes, and boots, shoes and feet grip differently on the stage floor. It is difficult for actors to remember that the technical and dress rehearsal will mean them wearing costume for much longer than at any other time during the run of the show. Because of this, and because of the lengthy hold-ups while lights, sound, rigging and other technical hitches are being resolved, they have time to think about their discomfort – all of which creates a demanding day or two for the designer and the costume department.

The actors need reassuring that their costumes are comfortable and safe. Small difficulties of fastenings and hems will become evident, and minor changes prove necessary. And there are times when a costume simply

The technical rehearsal: (left) on stage (photo: Nik Mackey); (above) in the auditorium.

does not work for an unforeseen reason: it may look dreadful in the light, not fasten smoothly enough during an unexpectedly quick change, or not cope, in some way or other, with the demands that the reality of performance puts upon it. If you are certain that this cannot be remedied by less drastic means you must bite your bullet very hard and quickly, and decide to redesign and remake it. Your only consolation will be relief that you have the contingency money squirrelled away in your budget to pay for it, and that however tired you and your team are, you can sleep after the first night.

It may be demanding, but for designer and makers it is the beginning of the time when their work starts to live. The clothes and objects they have been seeing in their imagination, rather than in the unhelpful light and against the muddled backdrop of the rehearsal room, begin to be presented in their theatrical reality. The performers move in the light, and the world which you have imagined for the audience to see begins to breathe.

The collaborative discussions that have punctuated rehearsals have melded the work of the costume, set, lighting and sound designers. Your own faults will glare at you, and impossible new ideas flood into your head, but it is a marvellous moment.

However marvellous, it will be followed by slogging work to resolve all problems before the dress rehearsal. This should be exactly like a performance but without the audience, other than the crew who are watching their own work. The designer and costume department will be looking from all the different audience viewpoints and noting everything that could look better or work more smoothly. These notes will be added to with comments from the director and the creative team and crew, and will be addressed before the first night.

By this point all the costumes will need washing, and there will be many notes on the list to be sorted out and crossed off before they are hung – clean, dry, ironed, and as perfect as you can get them – in the dressing rooms ready for the actors to wear for the opening show. It is a special moment for all performers when they prepare in their dressing rooms for a first night. They are putting on or climbing into their roles as well as their costumes, and the orderly arrangement of costume and props helps them have confidence and to concentrate their minds and bodies into this adrenalin-filled hour.

Your particular moment comes later, when you sit with the audience and watch with them the world you imagined become real.

Index